MULTIPLE CHOICE QUESTIONS TO PREPARE FOR THE AP CALCULUS BC EXAM

(Third edition)

By Rita Korsunsky

Copyright © 2020 by Rita Korsunsky

All rights reserved.

ISBN: 9798644142675

No part of this book may be reproduced or transmitted in any form or by any means,
including electronic transmission and photocopying.

PREFACE

I am delighted to offer this book, titled "MULTIPLE CHOICE QUESTIONS TO PREPARE FOR THE AP CALCULUS BC EXAM ".

This book consists of two parts. The first part contains six sample multiple-choice exams. Section I Part A consists of 30 multiple-choice questions to be answered without the use of a calculator. Section 1 part B consists of 15 multiple-choice questions where a graphing calculator could be used. The second part of this book contains a comprehensive list of definitions, formulas and theorems, and tips for the AP test.

The sole purpose of this book is to help you prepare for the AP Calculus BC exam. On the exam, you will have to respond to both multiple-choice and free-response questions. It is my belief that extensive practice with multiple-choice questions will help to prepare you well for both sections.

Do not forget to practice for the free response part of the test. I strongly suggest that you practice by answering the free response questions from past AP tests. These are available for free on the College Board's website.

Completing the multiple choice tests offered in this book will enable you to learn your strengths and weaknesses. You will find out what material you need to review. If you focus on learning, re-learning, and reviewing this material, you will greatly improve your performance on the test.

There is no substitute for practice. Taking multiple practice tests will teach you what your problem areas are, and will increase your confidence on the day of the exam.

I would like to thank all of my past, present, and future students for inspiring me to publish this Book. A special thanks to Catherine Hwu and Amanda Zhu for hand drawing the exquisite book cover for the third edition of my book. I also wish to thank my sons David and Boris for their technical assistance and support. A special debt of gratitude is due to my husband Alex for his continual support and help every step of the way.

Please send all questions and concerns to:

captain@mathboat.com

Sincerely,

Rita Korsunsky

If you wish to order the solutions with step-by-step explanations to each and every problem made in a form of PowerPoint presentation, please visit www.mathboat.com

www.mathboat.com

TABLE OF CONTENTS

Examination I

Directions: Solve each of the following problems, using the space provided. Choose the best answer. Do not spend too much time on any one problem. Calculators may NOT be used on this part of the exam.

In this Exam: (1) Unless otherwise specified, the domain of a function is assumed to be the set of all real numbers x for which $f(x)$ is a real number.

(2) The inverse of a trigonometric function f may be indicated using the inverse function notation f^{-1} or with the prefix "arc" (e.g., $\sin^{-1}x = \arcsin x$)

1. What is the absolute maximum of the function $f(x) = \dfrac{1}{2}x^4 - \dfrac{4}{3}x^3 + 2$ on the interval $[-1, 3]$?

(A)3   (B)$\dfrac{23}{6}$ (C)$\dfrac{13}{2}$ (D)$\dfrac{17}{2}$

$2x^3 - 4x^2$

$2x^2(x-2)$

$x=0 \quad x=2$

$f'(x) \quad \dfrac{-}{0} \dfrac{-}{} \dfrac{+}{2}$

Answer_____

2. $\displaystyle\lim_{x\to\pi}\dfrac{\cos^3\left(\dfrac{x}{2}\right)}{\sin x} = \dfrac{(\cos(\frac{x}{2}))^3}{\cos x}$

$= \dfrac{\frac{1}{2}\cos(\frac{x}{2})\cdot - \sin(\frac{x}{2})\cdot 3\left(\cos^2(\frac{x}{2})\right)}{\cos x} = \dfrac{-1}{-1}$

(A) 0   (B) $\dfrac{1}{2}$ (C) $\dfrac{2}{3}$ (D) 1

Answer ___D___

Unauthorized copying of this page is illegal

3. A curve is defined by the parametric equations $x(t) = 5e^{6t}$ and $y(t) = e^{3t+6} + 6$.

What is $\dfrac{d^2 y}{dx^2}$ in terms of t?

$\dfrac{dy}{dx} = \dfrac{3e^{3t+6}}{30e^{6t}}$

$(A)\ \dfrac{-3e^{-3t+6}}{10}$

$= \dfrac{e^{3t+6}}{10e^{6t}} = \dfrac{e^{-3t+6}}{10}$

$(B)\ -\dfrac{e^{-9t+6}}{100}$

$(C)\ \dfrac{e^{-9t+6}}{600}$

$\dfrac{d^2 y}{dx^2} = \dfrac{-3e^{-3t+6}}{10(30(e^{6t}))}$

$(D)\ -\dfrac{e^{-9t+6}}{60}$

Answer ___B___

4. Let the function $f(x)$ be continuos for all x. The figure below shows the graph of $f''(x)$.

Which of the following statements about $f(x)$ or $f'(x)$ must be true?

I. f has a relative maximum in the open interval $c < x < d$.

II. f is concave up for $x < a$ and $b < x < c$.

III. f' has a relative minimum in the open interval $a < x < c$

(A) II only (B) III only (C) II and III only (D) I, II, and III

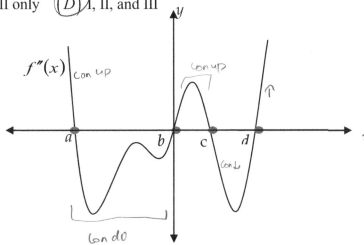

$f''(x)$ Con up   Con up

Con do   Con do

Answer ___D___

Unauthorized copying of this page is illegal

5. Which of the three series below converge?

I. $\displaystyle\sum_{n=2}^{\infty} \frac{1}{n}$ II. $\displaystyle\sum_{n=2}^{\infty} \frac{\ln n}{n}$ III. $\displaystyle\sum_{n=2}^{\infty} \frac{(\ln n)^2}{n}$

(A) None (B) II only (C) III only (D) I and III

Answer_____

6. Which of the following integral expressions is equal to $\displaystyle\lim_{n\to\infty} \sum_{k=1}^{n} \left(\sqrt{3+\frac{4k}{n}} \cdot \frac{1}{n} \right)$?

$(A) \displaystyle\int_0^4 \sqrt{3+4x}\; dx$ $(B) \displaystyle\int_3^7 \sqrt{3+4x}\; dx$ $(C) \dfrac{1}{4}\displaystyle\int_3^7 \sqrt{x}\; dx$ $(D) \displaystyle\int_3^7 \sqrt{x}\; dx$

Answer_____

7. The graph of the function $f(x)$, consisting of two line segments, is shown in the figure below. Let g be the function given by $g(x) = x^2 + x - 1$, and let h be the function given by $h(x) = f(g(x))$. What is the value of $h'(1)$?

$(A)\ 5$ $(B)\ \dfrac{5}{3}$ $(C)\ 3$ $(D)\ \dfrac{3}{5}$

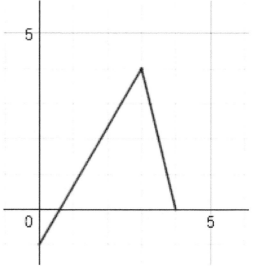

Answer_____

8. If $f(x) = \tan\left(\ln(5x)\right)$, then $f'(x) =$

$(A)\dfrac{-\sec^2\left(\ln(5x)\right)}{5x}$

$(B)\dfrac{\sec^2\left(\ln(5x)\right)}{5x}$

$(C)\dfrac{\sec^2\left(\ln(5x)\right)}{x}$

$(D) -5\sec^2\left(\ln(5x)\right)$

Answer _____

Unauthorized copying of this page is illegal

Examination I

9. The graphs of functions f and g are shown below. The value of $\lim\limits_{x \to 2} g(f(x))$ is:

$(A)\,0 \quad (B)\,1 \quad (C)\,2 \quad (D)\,3$

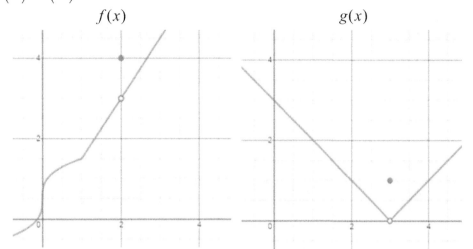

f(x)   g(x)

Answer_____

---

10. Which of the following integrals is equal to the length of the curve $x = \dfrac{15y^3 - 2y - 1}{8}$ from $A(5,\ 1.43)$ to $B(10,\ 1.78)$?

$(A)\ \displaystyle\int_{1.43}^{1.78} \sqrt{\dfrac{45y^2}{8} + \dfrac{3}{4}}\,dy$

$(B)\ \displaystyle\int_{1.43}^{1.78} \sqrt{1 + \left(\dfrac{45y^2}{8} - \dfrac{1}{4}\right)^2}\,dy$

$(C)\ \displaystyle\int_{5}^{10} \sqrt{1 + \left(15y^3 - 2y - 1\right)^2}\,dy$

$(D)\ \displaystyle\int_{1.43}^{1.78} \sqrt{1 + \left(\dfrac{45y^2}{8} - \dfrac{1}{2}\right)^2}\,dy$

Answer_____

Unauthorized copying of this page is illegal

x	0	1	2	3
$f(x)$	-5	-3	1	7
$f'(x)$	2	1	4	5

11. The table above gives selected values of a differentiable and increasing function f and its derivative. If g is the inverse function of f, what is the value of $g'(1)$?

$(A)\ \dfrac{1}{4}$ $(B)\ \dfrac{1}{3}$ $(C)\ \dfrac{1}{2}$ $(D)\ 1$

Answer_____

12. $\displaystyle\int_{1}^{2}\left(1+\frac{1}{x}\right)^{-2}\left(\frac{1}{x^2}\right)dx =$

$(A)\ \dfrac{1}{2}$ $(B)\ \dfrac{1}{6}$ $(C)\ \dfrac{1}{12}$ $(D)\ \dfrac{1}{3}$

Answer_____

Unauthorized copying of this page is illegal

13. The slope of function $y = f(x)$ is given by $6x^4 - 12x^2 + 2$. What are the x-coordinates of all points of inflections of $y = f(x)$?

$(A) -\dfrac{\sqrt{3}}{3}, \dfrac{\sqrt{3}}{3}$

$(B) \ -1, 1$

$(C) \ 0, 1$

$(D) \ -1, 0, 1$

Answer_____

14. If $\displaystyle\lim_{x \to 3} \dfrac{f(x)}{2x - 6} = f'(3) = 0$, which of the following must be true?

(A) I only   I. $(3, 0)$ is a critical point of $f(x)$

                  II. $f(x)$ has a local maximum at $x = 3$

(B) III only   III. $f(x)$ is continuous at $x = 3$

(C) I and III only

(D) I, II, and III

Answer _____

Unauthorized copying of this page is illegal

15. Let $y = f(x)$ be the particular solution to the differential equation $\dfrac{dy}{dx} = \dfrac{Mx - 4y}{(x+1)}$

with the initial condition $f(0) = 1$ where M is a constant. Euler's method, starting

at $x = 0$ with a step size of 3, is used to approximate $f(6)$.

The initial and final steps of this approximation are shown in the table below.

What is the value of M?

(A) 14/9

(B) 16/3

(C) −7

(D) −4/9

$x_0 = 0$		$x_2 = 6$
$f(x_0) = 1$		$f(x_2) \approx 21$

Answer_____

16. $\displaystyle\int_0^{\pi} x\cos 3x \, dx =$

(A) $-\dfrac{2}{9}$

(B) 0

(C) $-\dfrac{2}{3}$

(D) $\dfrac{2}{9}$

Answer _____

Unauthorized copying of this page is illegal

17. If the function f defined by $f(x) = \begin{cases} 1 + e^{-2x}, & 0 \le x \le b \\ 1 + e^{2x-12}, & b < x \le 6 \end{cases}$

is continuous for all values of x on the interval $[0,6]$, which of the following is the value of b?

(A) 1 (B) 2 (C) 3 (D) 4

Answer_____

18. The convergent power series in x that has the sum equal to $\dfrac{x^3}{2 - x^3}$ when $|x| < \sqrt[3]{2}$ is

$(A) \dfrac{1}{2} \displaystyle\sum_{n=0}^{\infty} \dfrac{x^{3n+3}}{2^n}$

$(B) \displaystyle\sum_{n=0}^{\infty} \dfrac{x^{3n+3}}{2^n}$

$(C) \dfrac{1}{2} \displaystyle\sum_{n=0}^{\infty} \dfrac{x^{3n}}{2^n}$

$(D) \dfrac{1}{2} \displaystyle\sum_{n=0}^{\infty} \dfrac{x^{3n+3}}{4^n}$

Answer _____

Unauthorized copying of this page is illegal

19. What is the slope of the tangent line to the curve $\left(x^3 + y\right)^2 - 2a^2 xy = b^2$ at the point $P\left(0,1\right)$ when $a = \sqrt{2}$ and $b = 1$?

$\left(A\right) - 2$

$\left(B\right) - \frac{1}{2}$

$\left(C\right)\ 2$

$\left(D\right)\frac{1}{2}$

Answer_____

20. A circle is inscribed in a square. The area of the circle is increasing at a constant rate of $15\pi\ \text{in}^2/\text{sec}$. As the circle expands, the square expands to keep the circle inscribed. At what rate is the area of the square increasing in in^2/sec?

$\left(A\right) 30 \quad \left(B\right)\ \frac{60}{\pi} \quad \left(C\right)\ \frac{120}{\pi} \quad \left(D\right) 60$

Answer _____

Unauthorized copying of this page is illegal

21. A boy runs on a straight road for $0 \le t \le 8$ seconds. The graph below, which consists of two line segments, shows the velocity, in meters per second, of the boy. What is the total distance, in meters, run by the boy over the time interval $0 \le t \le 8$ seconds?

(A) 70

(B) 70.5

(C) 71

(D) 71.5

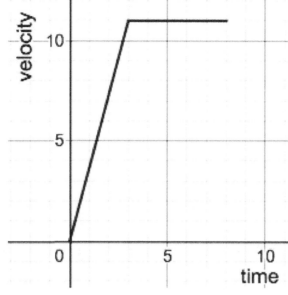

Answer_____

x	0	5	10	15	20
$f(x)$	1	4	8	13	19
$f'(x)$	1	2	3	6	24

22. The table above gives values of a differentiable function f and its derivatives at selected values of x. If h is the function given by $h(x) = f(5x)$, which of the following statements must be true?

(I) There exists c, where $1 < c < 3$, such that $h(c) = 10$.

(II) There exists c, where $0 < c < 3$, such that $h'(c) = 4$.

(III) h is increasing on $2 < x < 3$.

(A) II only

(B) I and II only

(C) II and III only

(D) I, II, and III

Answer _____

Unauthorized copying of this page is illegal

23. Which of the following is a power series expansion for $\dfrac{e^{-3x} + e^{3x}}{6x}$?

$(A)\dfrac{1}{3x} - \dfrac{3x}{2!} + \dfrac{(3x)^3}{4!} - \dfrac{(3x)^5}{6!} + \ldots + (-1)^n \dfrac{(3x)^{2n-1}}{(2n)!} + \ldots$ $(B)\dfrac{1}{3x} + \dfrac{3x}{2!} + \dfrac{(3x)^3}{4!} + \dfrac{(3x)^5}{6!} + \ldots + \dfrac{(3x)^{2n-1}}{(2n)!} + \ldots$

$(C)1 + \dfrac{(3x)^2}{3!} + \dfrac{(3x)^4}{5!} + \dfrac{(3x)^6}{7!} + \ldots + \dfrac{(3x)^{2n}}{(2n+1)!} + \ldots$ $(D)1 - \dfrac{(3x)^2}{3!} + \dfrac{(3x)^4}{5!} - \dfrac{(3x)^6}{7!} + \ldots + (-1)^n \dfrac{(3x)^{2n}}{(2n+1)!} + \ldots$

Answer_____

24. Shown on the right is the slope field for which differential equation?

$(A)\quad \dfrac{dy}{dx} = 2x$

$(B)\quad \dfrac{dy}{dx} = 2x - 4$

$(C)\quad \dfrac{dy}{dx} = 4 - 2x$

$(D)\quad \dfrac{dy}{dx} = x + y$

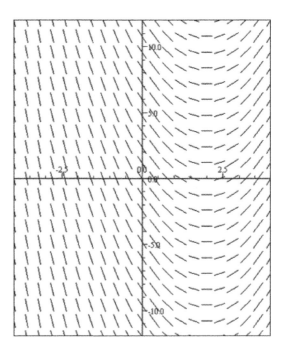

Answer _____

Unauthorized copying of this page is illegal

25. Consider the curve given by parametric equations: $x = 3t^4 - 2t^2$ and $y = t^4 - 5t$. What is $\dfrac{dy}{dx}$ at $t = 1$?

$(A) -\dfrac{2}{7}$ $(B) -\dfrac{1}{8}$ $(C) -\dfrac{7}{2}$ $(D) -8$

Answer_____

26. What are all values of p for which $\displaystyle\int_{1}^{\infty}\left(\dfrac{1}{x^{2p+3}}\right)dx$ converges?

$(A)\ p \geq -0.5$

$(B)\ p > -0.5$

$(C)\ p < -1$

$(D)\ p > -1$

Answer_____

Unauthorized copying of this page is illegal

27. Let g be a function such that $g'(x) = \cos(x^4)$ and $g(0) = 5$. What are the first five nonzero terms of the Maclaurin series for g?

$(A)\ 5 + x - \dfrac{x^9}{9(2!)} + \dfrac{x^{17}}{17(4!)} - \dfrac{x^{25}}{25(6!)}$

$(B)\ 5 - \dfrac{x^8}{(2!)} + \dfrac{x^{16}}{(4!)} - \dfrac{x^{24}}{(6!)} + \dfrac{x^{32}}{(8!)}$

$(C)\ 5 + x - \dfrac{8x^7}{(2!)} + \dfrac{16x^{15}}{(4!)} - \dfrac{24x^{23}}{(6!)}$

$(D)\ 5 + x - \dfrac{x^7}{7(2!)} + \dfrac{x^{15}}{15(4!)} - \dfrac{x^{23}}{23(6!)}$

Answer_____

28. If $f'(x) = \lim\limits_{h \to 0} \dfrac{(x+h)^3 - x^3}{h}$, which of the following must be true:

      I. $f'(x) \leq 0$ for all x

      II. $f'(x) \geq 0$ for all x

      III. $f(x)$ is concave down when $x \geq 0$

(A) I only

(B) II only

(C) III only

(D) II and III only

Answer_____

Unauthorized copying of this page is illegal

29. Using the table below, what is $\left(\dfrac{f}{g}\right)'(3)$?

(A) $-\dfrac{2}{3}$

(B) $-\dfrac{2}{27}$

$f(3)$	$g(3)$	$f'(3)$	$g'(3)$
7	-9	-4	6

(C) $\dfrac{2}{3}$

(D) $\dfrac{2}{27}$

Answer_____

30. The graph of f'', the second derivative of f, is the line shown in the figure below. If $f'(0) = 2.5$, then $f'(2) =$

(A) 9.5

(B) 10.5

(C) 11.0

(D) 11.5

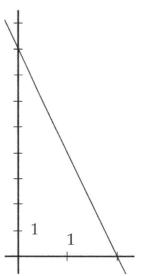

$y = f''(x)$

Answer_____

Unauthorized copying of this page is illegal

Examination I

Directions: Solve each of the following problems, using the space provided. Choose the best answer. Do not spend too much time on any one problem.

A graphing calculator is required for some questions on this part of the exam.

In this Exam:

(1) The exact numerical value of the correct answer does not always appear among the choices given. Then select from among the choices the number that best approximates the exact numerical value.

(2) Unless otherwise specified, the domain of a function is assumed to be the set of all real numbers x for which $f(x)$ is a real number.

(3) The inverse of a trigonometric function f may be indicated using the inverse function notation f^{-1} or with the prefix "arc" (e.g., $\sin^{-1} x = \arcsin x$)

---

31. Which of the following is the radius of convergence of the series $\displaystyle\sum_{n=0}^{\infty} \frac{(-1)^n n! x^n}{n^n}$?

$(A)\dfrac{1}{e}$ $(B)1$ $(C)e$ $(D)\infty$

Answer _____

32. The composition of two functions, $h(x) = f(g(x))$ is a differentiable function. Using the tables below what is the approximate value of the derivative of $h(x)$ at $x = 1.35$?

(A) 15.88 (B) 10.72 (C) 3.97 (D) 13.29

x	2.5	2.7	2.9
$f'(x)$	3.85	3.97	4.03

x	1.30	1.35	1.40
$g(x)$	2.5	2.7	2.9

Answer_____

33. If f is an antiderivative of $\dfrac{\sin^2 x}{x^2 + 2}$ such that $f(2) = \dfrac{1}{2}$, then $f(0) = ?$

(A) -0.325

(B) 0.175

(C) 0.825

(D) 1.175

Answer _____

Unauthorized copying of this page is illegal

34. What is the length of the curve given by the pair of parametric equations $x = \cos 3t$ and $y = \sin^3 t$ from $t = \pi$ to $t = 3\pi$?

(A) 12.513 (B) 13.262 (C) 14.563 (D) 15.827

Answer_____

35. The function $f(x) = \sin x$ is defined on the interval $[0, b]$. The line tangent to the graph of $f(x)$ at $x = 1.531$ is parallel to the segment connecting the endpoints of $[0, b]$. What is the value of b?

(A) 2.704

(B) 4.787

(C) 3.567

(D) 3.021

Answer_____

Unauthorized copying of this page is illegal

36. Water is being pumped continuously from a water pool at a rate proportional to the amount of water left in the pool; that is, $\dfrac{dy}{dt} = ky$, where y is the amount of water left in the pool at any time t. Initially there were 500,000 gallons of water in the pool, and 10 days later there were 100,000 gallons left. What is the equation for y, the amount of water remaining in the pool at any time t?

$(A)\ y(t) = 500,000 e^{\frac{1}{5}t}$

$(B)\ y(t) = 500,000 \left(\dfrac{1}{10}\right)^{\frac{t}{10}}$

$(C)\ y(t) = 500,000 \cdot \left(\dfrac{1}{5}\right)^{\frac{t}{10}}$

$(D)\ y(t) = 500,000 e^{10t}$

Answer_____

37. The table below gives values of the continuous function $f(x)$ at selected values of x. Which of the following intervals must contain a solution to $f(x) = 7$?

x	−8	2	4	5
$f(x)$	0	6	12	8

$(A)\ [-8, 2]$

$(B)\ [2, 4]$

$(C)\ [4, 5]$

$(D)\ $ none of the above

Answer_____

Unauthorized copying of this page is illegal

38. The position of an object moving along a path in the xy-plane is given by the parametric equations $x(t) = 4\cos\left(\dfrac{\pi t}{3}\right)$ and $y(t) = (5t-3)^3$. The speed of the particle at time $t = 4$ is

(A) 4335

(B) 4339

(C) 4356

(D) 4361

Answer_____

39. What is the average value of the function $G(x) = 30 - \dfrac{x^8}{2,500,000}$ on the interval where $G(x) \geq 0$?

(A) 28.473

(B) 27.134

(C) 26.667

(D) 25.431

Answer_____

Unauthorized copying of this page is illegal

40. The region bounded by the graphs of the equations $y = 5$ and $5x^4 - y = 3x^2 - 3$ is revolved around the x-axis. What is the approximate volume of the resulting solid?

(A) 31.416

(B) 68.793

(C) 81.274

(D) 98.696

Answer_____

41. A particle moving in the xy-plane has velocity vector given by $v(t) = <e^{\cos t}, 3t^2>$ for time $t \geq 0$. What is the magnitude of the displacement of the particle between times $t = 2$ and $t = 3$?

(A) 7.132 (B) 10.982 (C) 19.006 (D) 19.105

Answer_____

Unauthorized copying of this page is illegal

42. The base of a solid is the region in the fourth quadrant enclosed by the graph of $y = x^2 - 9$ and the coordinate axes. If every cross section perpendicular to the x-axis is a square, then the volume of the solid is

$(A)64.8$ $(B)129.6$ $(C)171.0$ $(D)194.4$

Answer_____

43. If $\int_{1}^{7} f(x)\,dx = 6$ and $\int_{7}^{1} g(x)\,dx = 12$ and $\int_{1}^{7} h(x)\,dx = \int_{1}^{5}(2f(x) - g(x))\,dx + \int_{7}^{5}(g(x) - 2f(x))\,dx,$

what is the average value of $h(x)$ on the interval $1 \le x \le 7$?

$(A)\,1$ $(B)\,2$ $(C)\,4$ $(D)\,12$

Answer _____

Unauthorized copying of this page is illegal

44. Let f be a function having derivatives of all orders for all real numbers x. The third-degree Taylor polynomial for f about $x = 4$ is given by $T(x) = \dfrac{1}{9} + 5(x-4)^2 - 8(x-4)^3$.

If $\left| f^{(4)}(x) \right| \le \dfrac{1}{4}$ for $3.5 \le x \le 4$, order the following from greatest to least.

I. Maximum value of $\left| T(x) - f(x) \right|$ for $3.5 \le x \le 4$ II. $\left| f''(4) \right|$ III. $\left| f(4) \right|$

(A) I, II, III

(B) II, I, III

(C) II, III, I

(D) III, II, I

Answer_____

45. Let R be the region that lies inside the polar curve $r = 2 - \cos\theta$ and also inside the polar curve $r = 1 + \cos\theta$. What is the area of R?

(A) 1.611 (B) 2.658 (C) 2.457 (D) 3.222

Answer_____

Unauthorized copying of this page is illegal

Examination II

Directions: Solve each of the following problems, using the space provided. Choose the best answer. Do not spend too much time on any one problem. Calculators may NOT be used on this part of the exam.

In this Exam: (1) Unless otherwise specified, the domain of a function is assumed to be the set of all real numbers x for which $f(x)$ is a real number.

(2) The inverse of a trigonometric function f may be indicated using the inverse function notation f^{-1} or with the prefix "arc" (e.g., $\sin^{-1} x = \arcsin x$)

1. Let f be defined as follows, where $a \neq 0$.

$$f(x) = \begin{cases} \dfrac{x^3 - a^3}{x^2 - a^2}, & \text{for } x \neq a \\ 1, & \text{for } x = a \end{cases}$$

Which of the following must be true about f ?

    I. $\lim\limits_{x \to a} f(x)$ exists

    II. $f(a)$ exists

    III. $f(x)$ is continuous at $x = a$

(A) I only (B) II only (C) I and II only (D) I, II, and III

Answer _____

2. The slope of a curve at point (x, y) is defined as $\lim\limits_{h \to 0} \dfrac{(x+h)^3 + (x+h)^2 - x^3 - x^2}{h}$. Which of the following is the equation of the tangent to this curve at $x = 1$?

$(A)\ y = 5x - 3$

$(B)\ y = 3x - 9$

$(C)\ y = 5x - 2$

$(D)\ y = 3x - 6$

Answer _____

Unauthorized copying of this page is illegal

3. The shaded region in the figure to the right is bounded by the graphs of $y = x^3 - 1$ and $y = 1 - x^4$ for $-1.544 \le x \le 1$. Which of the following expressions gives the perimeter of the region?

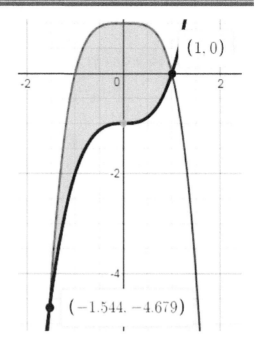

(1,0)

$(-1.544, -4.679)$

(A) $\int_{-1.544}^{1} \sqrt{1 + \left(x^3 - 1\right)^2}\, dx + \int_{-1.544}^{1} \sqrt{1 + \left(1 - x^4\right)^2}\, dx$

(B) $2\int_{-1.544}^{1} \sqrt{x^3 - x^4}\, dx$

(C) $\int_{-1.544}^{1} \sqrt{1 + 9x^4}\, dx + \int_{-1.544}^{1} \sqrt{1 + 16x^6}\, dx$

(D) $\int_{-1.544}^{1} \sqrt{9x^4 + 16x^6}\, dx$

Answer_____

4. If $f(x) = g(h(x))$ and if $h(2) = 5$, $h'(2) = -5$, $g'(5) = 3$ which of the following is $f'(2)$?

(A) 3

(B) -15

(C) 15

(D) -3

Answer_____

Unauthorized copying of this page is illegal

5. Which of the following is y', the first derivative of the function $y = f(x)$ if $x^2 y + \sec y = 8$?

$(A)\ -2xy \cdot \left(x^2 \sec y \tan y \right)$ $(B)\ \dfrac{x^2 y}{\sec y \tan y}$ $(C)\ \dfrac{-2xy}{x^2 - \sec y \tan x}$ $(D)\ \dfrac{-2xy}{x^2 + \sec y \tan y}$

Answer_____

6. If $f(x) = 6x^2 + 4x$, what is the number c in the interval $\left[0, 4 \right]$ such that the line tangent to the graph of $f(x)$ at the point $x = c$ is parallel to the line drawn through the endpoints of the interval?

$(A)\ \dfrac{5}{3}$

$(B)\ 4$

$(C)\ \dfrac{3}{5}$

$(D)\ 2$

Answer_____

7. Which of the following series are absolutely convergent?

$(A) \sum_{n=1}^{\infty} (-1)^{n+1} \dfrac{1}{n+3}$

$(B) \sum_{n=1}^{\infty} (-1)^{n+1} \dfrac{n^2}{5n^2+100}$

$(C) \sum_{n=1}^{\infty} (-1)^{n+1} \dfrac{1}{n^2+2}$

$(D) \sum_{n=1}^{\infty} (-1)^{n+1} \left(\dfrac{4}{3}\right)^n$

Answer_____

8. $\int x^2 \sec^2\left(x^3\right) dx =$

$(A) \dfrac{1}{3}\tan^2\left(x^3\right) + C$

$(B) \ 3\tan\left(x^3\right) + C$

$(C) \ 3\sec\left(x^3\right) + C$

$(D) \dfrac{1}{3}\tan\left(x^3\right) + C$

Answer_____

Unauthorized copying of this page is illegal

9. For which of the following values of k do both $\sum_{n=1}^{\infty}\left(\dfrac{3}{k}\right)^{n}$ and $\sum_{n=1}^{\infty}\dfrac{(3-k)^{n}}{\sqrt{n+3}}$ converge?

(A) 2

(B) 3

(C) 4

(D) 5

Answer_____

10. Let f be the function given by $f(x) = e^{2x}$ for $-\infty < x \le 0$ and let R be the region between the graph of f and the x-axis. Which of the following is equal to the area of the region R?

(A) $\dfrac{1}{4}$

(B) $\dfrac{1}{2}$

(C) 1

(D) The area is infinite

Answer_____

Unauthorized copying of this page is illegal

Examination II

11. The figure below shows the graph of f', the derivative of the function f, on the closed interval $-1 \leq x \leq 5$. The graph of f' has horizontal tangent lines at $x=1$ and $x=3$. The function f is twice differentiable with $f(3)=8$. Let g be the function defined by $g(x)=x^2 f(x)$. Which of the following is the equation for the line tangent to the graph of g at $x=3$?

$(A)\ y-24=72(x+3)$

$(B)\ y-9=21(x-3)$

$(C)\ y-72=21(x-3)$

$(D)\ y-36=14(x-3)$

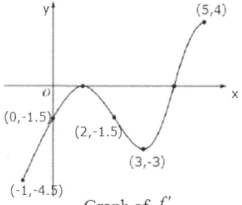

Graph of f'

Answer_____

12. The graph of the function h is shown below. If g is the function given by $g(x) = h(h(x))$, what is the value of $g'(1)$?

$(A)\ -6$

$(B)\ -2$

$(C)\ 3$

$(D)\ -3$

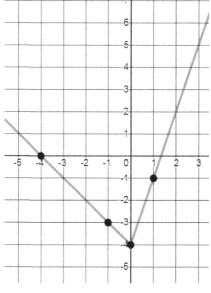

graph of $h(x)$

Answer _____

Unauthorized copying of this page is illegal

13. The Taylor series about $x = 2$ for a certain function f converges to $f(x)$ for all x in the interval of convergence. Then nth derivative of f at $x = 2$ is given by $f^{(n)}(2) = \dfrac{2^n n!}{3^{n+1}(n+1)}$ and $f(2) = 3$.

Which of the following is the radius of convergence for the Taylor series for f about $x = 2$?

$(A)\ \dfrac{2}{3}$ $(B)\ 0$ $(C)\ \dfrac{3}{2}$ $(D)\ 3$

Answer_____

14. The volume of the solid formed by revolving the region bounded by the graphs of $y = x^2 + 2$, $y = x + 1$, $x = 0$, and $x = 1$ about the horizontal line $y = 4$ is given by which of the following?

$(A)\ \pi\displaystyle\int_0^1\left((3-x)^2 - (2-x^2)^2\right)dx$

$(B)\ \pi\displaystyle\int_0^1\left((x+1)^2 - (x^2+2)^2\right)dx$

$(C)\ \pi\displaystyle\int_0^1\left((2-x^2)^2 - (3-x)^2\right)dx$

$(D)\ \pi\displaystyle\int_0^1\left((3-x)^2 - (6-x^2)^2\right)dx$

Answer_____

Unauthorized copying of this page is illegal

15. Shown below is the slope field of the differential equation. What could be the solution to this differential equation?

$(A)\, y = x^3$

$(B)\, y = -5x^2$

$(C)\, y = x$

$(D)\, y = x^2$

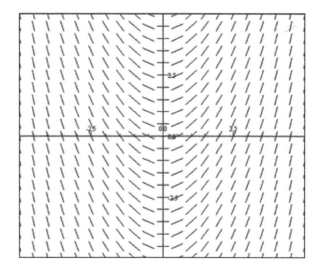

Answer_____

16. The 4th degree Maclaurin polynomial for the function g is $M_4(x) = 7 - 4x + 9x^2 + 2x^3 - 5x^4$.

Which of the following tables gives the values of second, third and fourth derivatives of g at $x = 0$?

$g''(x)$	$g'''(x)$	$g^{(4)}(x)$
18	12	-20

$g''(x)$	$g'''(x)$	$g^{(4)}(x)$
18	12	-24

$g''(x)$	$g'''(x)$	$g^{(4)}(x)$
18	12	-120

$g''(x)$	$g'''(x)$	$g^{(4)}(x)$
9	2	-5

Answer _____

Unauthorized copying of this page is illegal

17. The graphs of the functions f and g are shown in thefigures below. Which of the following statements is false?

(A) $\lim\limits_{x \to 2} f(x) = 1$

(B) $\lim\limits_{x \to 3} g(x)$ does not exist

(C) $\lim\limits_{x \to 2} (f(x)g(x+2))$ does not exist

(D) $\lim\limits_{x \to 2} (f(x+1)g(x))$ exists

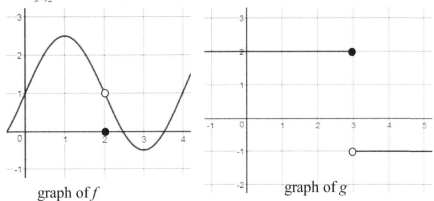

graph of f graph of g

Answer_____

18. Which of the following is equal to the area of the region bounded by the lines $x = -3, x = 1$, $y = 0$ and the curve $y = \dfrac{x+22}{x^2+2x-8}$ graphed below ?

$(A)\ln 5$ $(B)6\ln 5$ $(C)7\ln 5$ $(D)8\ln 5$

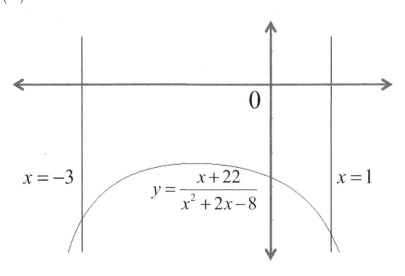

Answer _____

Unauthorized copying of this page is illegal

19. What are y coordinates of the points where $y^3 + x^2 + 30y^2 = 4x + 3$ has vertical tangent lines?

$(A)\ y = 0$ $\quad$ $(B)\ y = -20$ $\quad$ $(C)\ y = 0$ and $y = -20$ $\quad$ $(D)\ y = -20$ and $y = 2$

Answer_____

20. The amount of points that a basketball player scores in a season is modeled by a differentiable function $P(y)$ where y is the player's age in years. Of the following, which is the best interpretation of $P'(30) = 60$?

(A) For a basketball player at around age 30, he is now making double the points he scored last year.

(B) A 30 year-old basketball player scores around 60 points per year.

(C) The basketball player will score 1800 points this year.

(D) The amount of points the basketball player at age 30 scores is increasing at rate of 60 points per year.

Answer _____

Unauthorized copying of this page is illegal

21. Let the rate of change of a number x with respect to time t be $\dfrac{dx}{dt} = e^{-5x+2}$. What is the rate of change of the reciprocal of $\dfrac{dx}{dt}$ with respect to t at the moment when $x = \dfrac{45}{6}$?

(A) 5

(B) $-e^{\frac{45}{6}}$

(C) $e^{-\frac{45}{12}}$

(D) -5

Answer_____

22. Which of the following graphs is the graph of a differentiable function $f(x)$ that satisfies the given conditions:

$f(3) = 2, f'(0) = f'(3) = f'(5) = 0,$
$f'(x) < 0$ if $x < 0$ or $3 < x < 5$?

(A)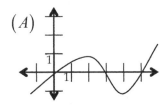

(B)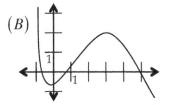

(C)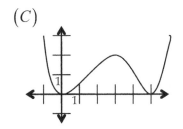

(D)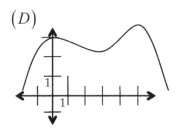

Answer_____

Unauthorized copying of this page is illegal

23. Function $f(x)$ is a linear function such that $f(x+2)-f(x)=8$. Given that $g(x)$ is the inverse of $f(x)$, which of the following is $g'(x)$?

$(A)\ \dfrac{1}{8}$

$(B)\ \dfrac{1}{4}$

$(C)\ \dfrac{1}{2}$

$(D)\ 4$

Answer_____

24. $\displaystyle\lim_{x\to 3}\dfrac{\displaystyle\int_{3}^{x}\cos\left(\dfrac{\pi t}{3}\right)dt}{x^{3}-27}=$

$(A)\ 0$

$(B)\ -\dfrac{1}{27}$

$(C)\ -3$

$(D)\ \dfrac{1}{27}$

Answer _____

Unauthorized copying of this page is illegal

25. The graph of $f'(x)$ shown has horizontal tangents at $(4,0)$ and $(12,-6)$. What are the $x-$coordinates for the point(s) of inflection of function $f(x)$?

(A) 4 only (B) 4 and 15 only (C) -3 and 20 only (D) 4 and 12 only

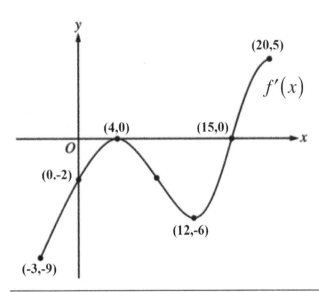

Answer_____

26. Let f be a function having derivatives of all orders for all real numbers. The third-degree Taylor polynomial for f about $x = 2$ is given by $T(x) = 5 - 9(x-2)^2 - 3(x-2)^3$.
$\left| f^{(4)}(x) \right| \le 9$ for all x in the interval $[0,2]$. Which of the following must be true?

I. The approximation for $f(0)$ using $T(x)$ is negative.

II. f has a critical point at $x = 0$.

III. $f(0)$ is negative.

(A) I only

(B) III only

(C) I and II only

(D) I and III only

Answer_____

Unauthorized copying of this page is illegal

27. If n is a positive integer, then $\lim\limits_{n\to\infty}\dfrac{1}{n}\left[\cos\dfrac{\pi}{n}+\cos\dfrac{2\pi}{n}+\ldots+\cos\dfrac{n\pi}{n}\right]$ can be expressed as

$(A)\displaystyle\int_0^1\cos\dfrac{\pi}{n}dx$ $(B)\pi\displaystyle\int_0^1\cos x\,dx$ $(C)\displaystyle\int_0^1\cos(\pi x)dx$ $(D)\displaystyle\int_0^\pi\cos\pi x\,dx\,?$

Answer_____

28. Which of the following can be shown to converge by the Limit Comparison test with

series $\displaystyle\sum_{n=1}^{\infty}\dfrac{1}{5^n}$?

$(A)\displaystyle\sum_{n=1}^{\infty}\dfrac{1}{5^n-n}$

$(B)\displaystyle\sum_{n=1}^{\infty}\dfrac{1}{6^n}$

$(C)\displaystyle\sum_{n=1}^{\infty}\dfrac{1}{5^n\ln n}$

$(D)\displaystyle\sum_{n=1}^{\infty}\dfrac{1}{n^{\frac{1}{5}}}$

Answer_____

Unauthorized copying of this page is illegal

29. What is the solution to the differential equation $\dfrac{dy}{dx} = y \sec x \tan x$ with the initial condition

$y\left(\dfrac{\pi}{3}\right) = 5e^2?$

$(A)\ y = \ln 5 - \sec x$

$(B)\ y = 5 \sec x \tan x$

$(C)\ y = 5e^{\sec x}$

$(D)\ y = e^{(5 + \sec x)}$

Answer_____

30. A solid has a circular base of radius 4. If every plane cross section perpendicular to the x-axis

is an equilateral triangle (area of an equilateral triangle $A = \dfrac{s^2 \sqrt{3}}{4}$, where s is the length of its side),

then the volume is

$(A)\ \dfrac{256}{3}$

$(B)\ \dfrac{64}{3}\sqrt{3}$

$(C)\ \dfrac{128}{3}\sqrt{3}$

$(D)\ \dfrac{256}{3}\sqrt{3}$

Answer_____

Unauthorized copying of this page is illegal

Examination II

Section I Part B

Directions: Solve each of the following problems, using the space provided. Choose the best answer. Do not spend too much time on any one problem.

A graphing calculator is required for some questions on this part of the exam.

In this Exam:

(1) The exact numerical value of the correct answer does not always appear among the choices given. Then select from among the choices the number that best approximates the exact numerical value.

(2) Unless otherwise specified, the domain of a function is assumed to be the set of all real numbers x for which $f(x)$ is a real number.

(3) The inverse of a trigonometric function f may be indicated using the inverse function notation f^{-1} or with the prefix "arc" (e.g., $\sin^{-1}x = \arcsin x$)

---

31. Consider the curves $r = 3\sin\theta$ and $r = 1 + \sin\theta$. Which of the following is the area of the region inside the curve $r = 3\sin\theta$ and outside the curve $r = 1 + \sin\theta$?

$(A)\ \dfrac{\pi}{2}$ $\quad(B)\ \dfrac{2\pi}{3}$ $\quad(C)\ \pi$ $\quad(D)\ 2\pi$

Answer _____

Unauthorized copying of this page is illegal

32. The derivative of the function f is given by $f'(x) = \cos\left(\dfrac{1}{2}x^3\right) - \dfrac{x^2}{10}$. At what values of x does f have a relative maximum on the interval $0 < x < 3$?

(A) 1.400, 2.184, 2.435, 2.883, and 2.967

(B) 2.318 and 2.926

(C) 2.184 and 2.883

(D) 1.400, 2.435, and 2.967

Answer_____

33. Let P be the partition of an interval $\left[2,6\right]$ determined by $\{2,4,5,6\}$. Using the Midpoint Riemann Sum, R_p, which of the following is the best approximation for the area under the curve of $f(x) = x^2 + 4$ on the interval $\left[2,6\right]$?

(A)63.25 (B)65.5 (C)75.25 (D)84.5

Answer_____

Unauthorized copying of this page is illegal

34. The position $s(t)$ of a point P moving along a line is given by the function $s(t) = 5t^3 - 2t^2 + 8$ with t in seconds and $s(t)$ in centimeters. What is the average velocity in cm/sec of point P on the time interval $[1, 1.4]$?

(A) 16.00

(B) 17.00

(C) 32.00

(D) 34.94

Answer_____

35. Line l is tangent to the graph of $y = \cos x$ at the point $(m, \cos m)$, where $\pi < m < 2\pi$. For what value of m does the line pass through the point $(6, 0)$?

(A) 3.317

(B) 3.526

(C) 3.725

(D) 3.914

Answer_____

Unauthorized copying of this page is illegal

Examination II

36. The rodent population in a village increases according to the equation $P(t)=400-250e^{-0.123t}$ for $t \geq 0$, t measured in months. This population will approach a limiting value as time goes on. During which month will the population reach a half of its limiting value?

(A) First (B) Second (C) Third (D) Fourth

Answer_____

37. The velocity vector $v(t)$ of a particle moving in the xy-plane is given by $(-4\cos t,-5\sin t)$ for $t \geq 0$. At $t=0$, the particle is at the point $(1,3)$. Which of the following is the position vector at $t=4$?

$(A)(-2.027,4.732)$

$(B)(4.027,-5.268)$

$(C)(-3.027,3.268)$

$(D)(4.027,-1.268)$

Answer_____

Unauthorized copying of this page is illegal

Examination II

38. A graph of a function consists of a line segment from the point $(0,10)$ to point $(8,8)$, another line segment from $(8,8)$ to $(12,8)$, and a third line segment from $(12,8)$ to $(20,0)$. What is the average value of this function on the interval $[0,20]$?

(A) 136

(B) 7

(C) $\dfrac{34}{5}$

(D) $\dfrac{127}{20}$

Answer_____

39. A reactor coolant tank is being filled with coolant at the rate of $400\sqrt[3]{t}$ gallons per hour with $t>0$ measured in hours. If the tank originally contained 200 gallons of coolant, how many gallons are in the tank after 8 hours?

(A) 800

(B) 4800

(C) 5000

(D) 6400

Answer _____

Unauthorized copying of this page is illegal

40. For $t \geq 0$, the velocity of a particle moving along the y-axis is given by
$v(t) = 3t^3 + 2t^2 - 11t - 10$. At what time t does the direction of motion of the particle change
from down to up?

(A) 1.5 (B) 2.0 (C) 2.5 (D) 3

Answer_____

41. A particle, initially at rest, moves along the $x-$axis so that its acceleration at any time is given
by $a(t) = 8t^2 - 6$. Which of the following is the total distance traveled by the particle within the
time interval $2 \leq t \leq 4$?

(A) $\dfrac{412}{3}$

(B) 148

(C) $\dfrac{340}{3}$

(D) 124

Answer _____

Examination II

42. On the diagram below, the cross section of a water tank that is being drained is an equilateral triangle. The area of the cross section of water, $A(t)$, is decreasing at a rate of $10\text{cm}^2/\text{min}$. Which of the following is the rate (in cm/min) at which length of its side s is changing when area of the triangle is 250 cm^2? (Area of an equilateral triangle is $A = \dfrac{s^2\sqrt{3}}{4}$)

(A) -0.240 (B) -0.481 (C) -0.832 (D) -0.951

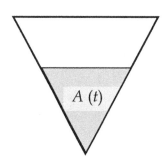

Answer_____

43. Let f be the function given by $f(t) = \dfrac{6}{1+t^3}$. Let G be the function given by $G(x) = \int\limits_{0}^{x} f(t)dt$.

Which of the following are the first 4 nonzero terms for the Taylor series expansion of $G(x)$ about $x = 0$?

(A) $-3x^2 + 6x^5 - 9x^8 + 27x^{11}$

(B) $-18x^2 + 36x^5 - 54x^8 + 72x^{11}$

(C) $6x - \dfrac{6x^4}{4} + \dfrac{6x^7}{7} - \dfrac{6x^{10}}{10}$

(D) $6 - 6x^3 + 6x^6 - 6x^9$

Answer _____

Unauthorized copying of this page is illegal

44. A pizza, heated to a temperature of 475 degrees Fahrenheit $\left(°F\right)$, is taken out of an oven and placed in a 105°F room at $t = 0$ minutes. The temperature of the pizza is changing at a rate of $-256e^{-0.7t}$ degrees Fahrenheit per minute. To the nearest degree, what is the temperature of the pizza at $t = 9$ minutes?

$\left(A\right)$ 110 $\left(B\right)$ 115 $\left(C\right)$ 120 $\left(D\right)$ 125

Answer_____

45. For $0 \le t \le 13$, a particle is moving along the x-axis and the velocity of the particle is

$v\left(t\right) = 4\cos\left(e^{\frac{t}{7}}\right)$. For what intervals is the particle's speed increasing?

$\left(A\right)$ $\left(0, 3.161\right) \cup \left(8.013, 10.851\right) \cup \left(12.865, 13\right)$

$\left(B\right)$ $\left(3.161, 8.013\right) \cup \left(12.865, 13\right)$

$\left(C\right)$ $\left(3.161, 8.013\right) \cup \left(10.851, 12.865\right)$

$\left(D\right)$ $\left(0, 3.161\right) \cup \left(10.851, 13\right)$

Answer_____

Unauthorized copying of this page is illegal

Examination III

Section I Part A

Directions: Solve each of the following problems, using the space provided. Choose the best answer. Do not spend too much time on any one problem. Calculators may NOT be used on this part of the exam.

In this Exam: (1) Unless otherwise specified, the domain of a function is assumed to be the set of all real numbers x for which $f(x)$ is a real number.

(2) The inverse of a trigonometric function f may be indicated using the inverse function notation f^{-1} or with the prefix "arc" (e.g., $\sin^{-1} x = \arcsin x$)

1. Let f be defined as follows,

$$f(x) = \begin{cases} x^2 + 1, & \text{for } -2 \le x < 2 \\ 1, & \text{for } x = 2 \\ 5, & \text{for } 2 < x < \infty \end{cases}$$

What is the limit of $f(x)$ as x approaches 2?

$(B)\ 1$ $(C)\ 2$ $(C)\ 5$ (D) nonexistent

Answer_____

2. What is the number represented by the difference between the average rate of change of function $y = f(x)$ with respect to x on the given interval $[1, 1.5]$ and the instantaneous rate of change of y with respect to x at the right endpoint of this interval if $y = 4x^2 - 1$?

$(A)\ 1$

$(B)\ 2$

$(C)\ 6$

$(D)\ 8$

Answer _____

Unauthorized copying of this page is illegal

3. $\lim\limits_{h \to 0} \dfrac{\cos\left(\dfrac{\pi}{3} + h\right) - \dfrac{1}{2}}{h} =$

$(A)\sqrt{3}$ $(B) -\dfrac{\sqrt{3}}{2}$ $(C) -\dfrac{1}{2}$ $(D) \dfrac{\sqrt{3}}{2}$

Answer_____

4. Given $xy^2 = 4$, what is the value of the second derivative of the function $y = f(x)$ at the point $(1,2)$?

$(A)\ \dfrac{3}{2}$

$(B)\ \dfrac{3}{4}$

$(C)\ 1$

$(D)\ \dfrac{1}{2}$

Answer _____

Unauthorized copying of this page is illegal

5. What is y if $\dfrac{dy}{dx} = \dfrac{3x+2}{5y}$ and $y = 1$ when $x = 2$?

$(A)\, y = \sqrt{\dfrac{3x^2 + 4x - 15}{5}}$ $(B)\, y = \pm\sqrt{\dfrac{3x^2 + 4x - 15}{5}}$

$(C)\, y = \pm\sqrt{\dfrac{3x^2 + 4x + 13}{2}}$ $(D)\, y = \sqrt{\dfrac{3x^2 + 4x}{5}}$

Answer_____

6. Which of the following definite integrals gives the length of the graph $y = e^{2x}$ between $x = 0$ and $x = 3$?

$(A)\, \displaystyle\int_0^3 \sqrt{1 + 4e^{4x}}\, dx$

$(B)\, \displaystyle\int_0^3 \sqrt{1 + e^{4x}}\, dx$

$(C)\, \displaystyle\int_0^3 \sqrt{1 + e^{2x}}\, dx$

$(D)\, \displaystyle\int_0^3 \sqrt{1 + 2e^{2x}}\, dx$

Answer_____

Unauthorized copying of this page is illegal

7. The figure below shows the graph of the derivative of a function f. How many points of inflection does f have in the interval shown on the diagram?

(A) Zero

(B) One

(C) Two

(D) More than two

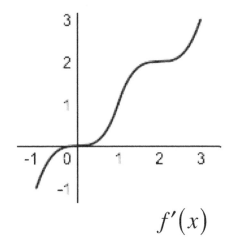

$f'(x)$

Answer_____

8. Which of the following is the maximum area of the rectangle that can be inscribed in a semicircle of radius $4\sqrt{2}$, if two vertices lie on the diameter?

(A) 24

(B) 32

(C) 36

(D) 64

Answer _____

Unauthorized copying of this page is illegal

9. Which of the following improper integrals diverge?

I. $\int\limits_{1}^{\infty}\dfrac{1}{x^{\frac{1}{3}}}dx$ II. $\int\limits_{0}^{\infty}\dfrac{1}{(x+2)^{2}}dx$ III. $\int\limits_{0}^{\infty}\dfrac{1}{e^{4x}}dx$

(A) I only

(B) II and III only

(C) I and II only

(D) I, II, and III

Answer_____

10. $\int\limits_{4}^{6}|x-5|dx =$

(A) 0

(B) 1

(C) 2

(D) 4

Answer_____

Unauthorized copying of this page is illegal

11. The Maclaurin series for $\ln(1+x)$ is given by $x - \dfrac{x^2}{2} + \dfrac{x^3}{3} - \dfrac{x^4}{4} + \cdots + (-1)^{n+1} \dfrac{x^n}{n} + \cdots$.

On its interval of convergence, this series converges to $\ln(1+x)$. Let f be the function

defined by $f(x) = x^2 \ln\left(1 + \dfrac{x}{4}\right)$. Which of the following expressions represents the

first three nonzero terms of the Maclaurin series for f?

$(A)\ \dfrac{x^3}{4} - \dfrac{x^4}{4^2} + \dfrac{x^5}{4^3} - \cdots$

$(B)\ \dfrac{x^2}{4} - \dfrac{x^3}{4^2} + \dfrac{x^4}{4^3} - \cdots$

$(C)\ \dfrac{x^3}{4} - \dfrac{x^4}{2 \cdot 4^2} + \dfrac{x^5}{3 \cdot 4^3} - \cdots$

$(D)\ \dfrac{x^3}{4^2} - \dfrac{x^4}{2 \cdot 4^3} + \dfrac{x^5}{2 \cdot 4^4} - \cdots$

Answer_____

12. The graph of $f(x)$ is shown below. List the following values of $f'(1), f'(-2), f''(0)$ from smallest to largest.

$(A)\ f'(-2),\ f''(0),\ f'(1)$

$(B)\ f''(0),\ f'(1),\ f'(-2)$

$(C)\ f''(0),\ f'(-2),\ f'(1)$

$(D)\ f'(1),\ f''(0),\ f'(-2)$

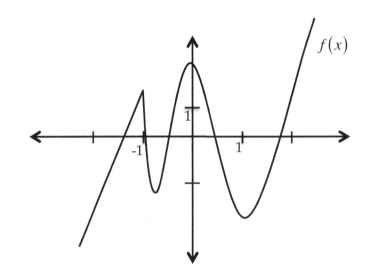

Answer_____

Unauthorized copying of this page is illegal

13. Consider the series $\sum_{n=0}^{\infty} (-1)^n a_n$, where $a_n > 0$ for all n. Which of the following

conditions does NOT guarantee that the series converges?

(A) $\sum_{n=0}^{\infty} b_n$ converges, where $b_n > a_n$ for all n

(B) $a_{n+1} < a_n$ for all n and $\lim_{n \to \infty} a_n = 0$

(C) $a_n = e^{-n}$

(D) $\sum_{n=0}^{\infty} (-1)^n a_n$ is a geometric series

Answer_____

14. The function $h(x) = \dfrac{f(x)}{g(x)}$ where $f(x)$ and $g(x)$ are piecewise linear functions whose graphs

are shown below. What is $h'(-2)$?

$(A) -\dfrac{3}{2}$ $(B) -1$ $(C) -\dfrac{1}{2}$ $(D) 1$

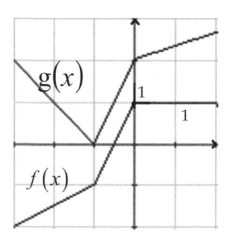

Answer _____

Unauthorized copying of this page is illegal

15. Given that $f(x)$ is a continuous function and $f(5)=9$ and $f(10)=3$. Which of the following is guaranteed by the Intermediate Value Theorem?

(A) $f(c)=7$ for at least one c between 3 and 9

(B) $f(c)=-2$ for at least one c between 3 and 9

(C) $f(c)=7$ for at least one c between 5 and 10

(D) $f(c)=-2$ for at least one c between 5 and 10

Answer_____

16. Given a series $\sum_{n=1}^{\infty} a_n = \sum_{n=1}^{\infty} \frac{6n(n^2+4)(n^3-3n+2)}{e^n(n^2+4n)(n^4-1)}$. When using the Limit Comparison Test with

$\sum_{n=1}^{\infty} b_n$, which choice of $\sum_{n=1}^{\infty} b_n$ would be appropriate to prove the convergence of $\sum_{n=1}^{\infty} a_n$?

(A) $\sum_{n=1}^{\infty} \frac{1}{n^2}$ (B) $\sum_{n=1}^{\infty} \frac{1}{n^3}$ (C) $\sum_{n=1}^{\infty} \frac{1}{ne^n}$ (D) $\sum_{n=1}^{\infty} \frac{1}{e^n}$

Answer _____

Unauthorized copying of this page is illegal

17. $\dfrac{d}{dx}\displaystyle\int_{4x}^{x^4}\left(t^4+2\right)^{11}dt =$

(A) $4x^3\left(\left(x^4\right)^4+2\right)^{11}-4\left(\left(4x\right)^4+2\right)^{11}$

(B) $\left(\left(x^4\right)^4+2\right)^{11}-\left(\left(4x\right)^4+2\right)^{11}$

(C) $4x^3\left(\left(x^4\right)^4+2\right)^{11}$

(D) $x^4\left(\left(x^4\right)^4+2\right)^{11}-4x\left(\left(4x\right)^4+2\right)^{11}$

Answer_____

18. What is the area of the region bounded by the curve $x = y^2 - 4$ and the y-axis?

(A) $\dfrac{28}{3}$

(B) 10

(C) $\dfrac{32}{3}$

(D) $\dfrac{34}{3}$

Answer_____

19. The population of giraffes is modeled by the function P that satisfies the differential equation $\dfrac{dP}{dt} = .05P(200 - P)$ where t is the time in years. Which of the following could be the slope field for this differential quation?

(A)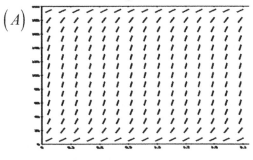

(B)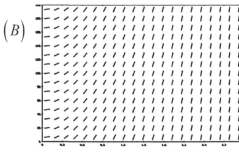

(C)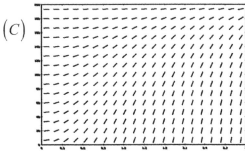

(D)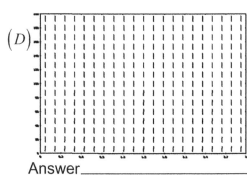

Answer_____

20. What is the derivative of function $y(x)$ if $\tan(2y) = xe^y$?

$(A) \dfrac{e^y}{2\sec^2(2y) - xe^y}$ $(B) \dfrac{e^y + xe^y}{2\sec^2(2y)}$ $(C) \dfrac{e^y}{\sec^2(2y) - xe^y}$ $(D) \dfrac{e^y}{2\sec(2y)\tan(2y) - xe^y}$

Answer _____

Unauthorized copying of this page is illegal

21. The series $1 - x^3 + \dfrac{x^6}{2!} - \dfrac{x^9}{3!} + \dfrac{x^{12}}{4!} + \ldots + (-1)^n \dfrac{x^{3n}}{n!} + \ldots$ converges to which of the following?

$(A)\cos x^3 - \sin x^3$

$(B)e^{-x^3} + 1$

$(C)e^{-x^3}$

$(D)\sin x^3$

Answer_____

---

22. What are all the values of x for which the series

$(x+1) - \dfrac{(x+1)^2}{2} + \dfrac{(x+1)^3}{3} - \ldots + \dfrac{(-1)^{n+1}(x+1)^n}{n} + \ldots$ converges?

$(A) -2 < x \leq 0$

(B) All real numbers

$(C) -2 < x < 0$

$(D) -2 \leq x \leq 0$

Answer _____

Unauthorized copying of this page is illegal

23. If n is a positive integer, then $\lim\limits_{n\to\infty}\dfrac{1}{n^3}\left[1^2+2^2+...+n^2\right]$ can be expressed as

$(A)\displaystyle\int_0^1 x^2\,dx$ $(B)\displaystyle\int_0^1\frac{1}{x}\,dx$ $(C)\displaystyle\int_0^1\frac{1}{x^3}\,dx$ $(D)\displaystyle\int_0^1 x^3\,dx$

Answer_____

24. What is $f'(x)$ if $f(x)=4^{\arctan\left(2x^5\right)}$?

$(A)\ 4^{\arctan\left(2x^5\right)}\cdot\sec^2\left(2x^5\right)\cdot\ln 4\cdot 10x^4$

$(B)\ 4^{\arctan\left(2x^5\right)}\cdot\dfrac{1}{\left(1+\left(2x^5\right)^2\right)\ln 4}\cdot 10x^4$

$(C)\ 4^{\arctan\left(2x^5\right)-1}\cdot\dfrac{10x^4}{1+\left(2x^5\right)^2}$

$(D)\ 4^{\arctan\left(2x^5\right)}\cdot\ln 4\cdot\dfrac{1}{1+\left(2x^5\right)^2}\cdot 10x^4$

Answer _____

Unauthorized copying of this page is illegal

25. $\lim\limits_{x\to 0} x^4 \sin\dfrac{1}{x^6}$ is

(A) 0

(B) 1

(C) π

(D) nonexistent

Answer_____

26. What is the slope of the line tangent to the polar curve $r = 2\cos\theta$ when $\theta = \dfrac{\pi}{3}$?

$(A)\dfrac{1}{2}$ $(B)\dfrac{\sqrt{3}}{3}$ $(C)-\sqrt{3}$ $(D)-\sqrt{2}$

Answer _____

Unauthorized copying of this page is illegal

27. Given the following, which of the functions $f, g,$ and h has at least one point of inflection?

  I. $f(x) = 2\sin 2x + 2$ II. $g'(x) = 5x^3$ III. $h(x) = \dfrac{6}{x} - \dfrac{1}{2x^2}$, $x \neq 0$

(A) I only

(B) II only

(C) I and II only

(D) I and III only

Answer_____

28. Shown on the right is the slope field for which differential equation?

(A) $\dfrac{dy}{dx} = \dfrac{y^2 - 2y}{x}$

(B) $\dfrac{dy}{dx} = \dfrac{3x^2 - 4}{x}$

(C) $\dfrac{dy}{dx} = \dfrac{3y^2 - 4}{4}$

(D) $\dfrac{dy}{dx} = \dfrac{y - 2}{2x}$

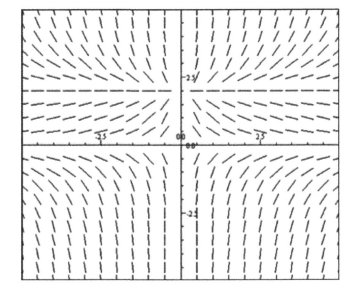

Answer _____

Unauthorized copying of this page is illegal

29. The quarter circle of radius 4 meters in the figure below represents the boundary of a small garden that is bordered by a path to the left. The flower density of the garden at a distance of x meters from the path is modeled by $D(x) = e^{4x} \tan x$, where $D(x)$ is measured in flowers per square meter. According to the model, which of the following expressions gives the total number of flowers in the garden?

(A) $\int_0^4 \sqrt{16-x^2}\, e^{4x} \tan x \, dx$

(B) $\int_0^4 (4-x) e^{4x} \tan x \, dx$

(C) $\int_0^4 4\sqrt{16-x^2}\, e^{4x} \tan x \, dx$

(D) $\int_0^4 x e^{4x} \tan x \, dx$

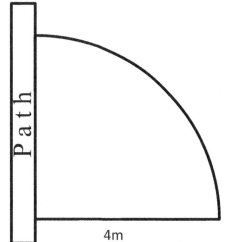

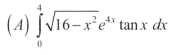

4m

Answer_____

30. Let function $f(x)$ be positive while its first derivative $f'(x)$, and its second derivative $f''(x)$ all be negative on a closed interval $[a,b]$. The interval $[a,b]$ is partitioned into n equal length sub-intervals and these are used to compute an Upper Sum U, a lower sum L, and the Trapezoidal Rule Approximation T. If $I = \int_a^b f(x)\,dx$, which statement below is true?

(A) $L < U < T < I$

(B) $L < T < I < U$

(C) $L < T < U < I$

(D) $L < I < T < U$

Answer _____

Unauthorized copying of this page is illegal

Examination III

Section I Part B

Directions: Solve each of the following problems, using the space provided. Choose the best answer.
Do not spend too much time on any one problem.
A graphing calculator is required for some questions on this part of the exam.

In this Exam:

(1) The exact numerical value of the correct answer does not always appear among the choices given.
Then select from among the choices the number that best approximates the exact numerical value.

(2) Unless otherwise specified, the domain of a function is assumed to be the set of all real numbers
x for which $f(x)$ is a real number.

(3) The inverse of a trigonometric function f may be indicated using the inverse function notation
f^{-1} or with the prefix "arc" (e.g., $\sin^{-1}x = \arcsin x$)

---

31. Let $f(x)$ be the function whose graph passes through the point $(0,1)$, and whose derivative
is given by $f'(x) = \dfrac{1+e^{2x}}{2x+1}$. What is the approximation of $f(1)$ if Euler's method is used starting
at $x = 0$ with the step size of 0.5?

$(A)\,2$ $(B)\,\dfrac{3+e}{4}$ $(C)\,\dfrac{9+e}{2}$ $(D)\,\dfrac{9+e}{4}$

Answer _____

Unauthorized copying of this page is illegal

32. As shown in the figure below the function $f(x)$ consists of a line segment from $(0,0)$ to $(3,5)$, another line segment from $(3,5)$ to $(7,5)$, and a quarter-circle with radius of 5. What approximately is the average value of this function on the interval $[0, 12]$?

(A) 3.470 (B) 3.511 (C) 3.928 (D) 41.635

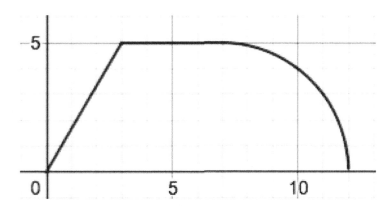

Answer_____

33. A particle moves along the $x-$axis so that at any time $t > 0$, its acceleration is given by $a(t) = \sin t - 3\sin t \cos t + 2t$. If the velocity of the particle is 6 m / sec at time $t = 3$ sec, then the velocity in m / sec of the particle at time $t = 7$ sec is approximately equal to

(A)43.639 (B)39.366 (C)37.639 (D)31.640

Answer_____

Unauthorized copying of this page is illegal

34. An object moves along the x – axis so that its position at any time t is given by

$x(t) = -4\cos\dfrac{t}{2} + 3$. For which value of t is its speed the greatest on the interval $[4,8]$?

$(A)\ t = 4$

$(B)\ t = 5$

$(C)\ t = 6$

$(D)\ t = 7$

Answer_____

35. An object moving along a curve at time t has position $(x(t), y(t))$ with $\dfrac{dx}{dt} = \cos(t^2)$

and $\dfrac{dy}{dt} = 2\sin(t^3)$ for $0 \le t \le 4$. At time $t = 2$ the object has position $(3,4)$.

Which of the following is the position of the object at time $t = 4$?

$(A)(2.574, 2.613)\quad (B)(3.133, 3.972)\quad (C)(4.052, 4.012)\quad (D)(3.133, 4.711)$

Answer _____

36. If f is a continuous function defined by

$$f(x) = \begin{cases} x^2 - bx, & x \le 3 \\ 3\cos\left(\dfrac{\pi}{4}x\right), & x > 3 \end{cases}$$

then $b \approx$

$(A) -2.2929$ $(B) 3.7071$ $(C) -3.7071$ $(D) 2.2929$

Answer_____

37. Let A be the region in the first quadrant bounded above by the graph $r = 5\cos\theta$ and bounded below by the graph $r = \theta$, as shown in the figure below. The two curves intersect when $\theta = 1.30$. What is the area of A?

(A) 0.447

(B) 0.389

(C) 0.471

(D) 0.503

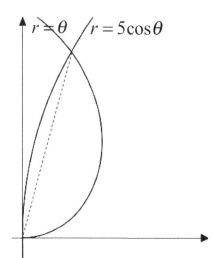

Answer _____

Unauthorized copying of this page is illegal

38. Which of the following is the equation of the line tangent to the curve described by the pair of parametric equations $x = 5t^3 - 5$ and $y = t^2 + 7$ at the point where $t = 2$?

(A) $15y - x = 130$

(B) $15y + x = 195$

(C) $10y + x = 145$

(D) $15y - 2x = 95$

Answer_____

39. Let the function $f(x) = \sin\left(4x + \dfrac{\pi}{6}\right)$, and let $P(x)$ be the third-degree Taylor polynomial for f about $x = 0$. What is the maximum value of $\left| f\left(\dfrac{1}{2}\right) - P\left(\dfrac{1}{2}\right) \right|$?

(A) 0.333

(B) 0.667

(C) 0.783

(D) 0.823

Answer _____

Unauthorized copying of this page is illegal

Examination III

40. A solid has its base the region bounded by the graph of $y = \dfrac{10}{1+x^2}$ and the horizontal line $y = 3$. What is the volume of the solid if every cross section by a plane perpendicular to the x-axis is a semicircle?

$(A)\,21.009 \quad (B)\,20.672 \quad (C)\,17.442 \quad (D)\,10.374$

Answer_____

41. A boy is standing on a dock watching a boat moving north away from him, at a speed of 5000ft / min. A girl is standing 1000 ft to the east of the boy and is watching the same boat. How fast is the boat moving away from the girl when it is 12500 ft away from the boy?

$(A)\,538.28 \quad (B)\,5023.94 \quad (C)\,4984.08 \quad (D)\,4321.95$

Answer_____

42. The region bounded by the graph of $y = -x^2 + 2$ and the x – axis is revolved around $y = 3$. What is the volume of the resulting solid?

(A) 52.130 (B) 27.842 (C) 24.600 (D) 12.506

Answer_____

43. The population $P(t)$ of a species satisfies the logistic differential equation $\dfrac{dP}{dt} = P\left(224 - \dfrac{P}{56}\right)$

where the initial population $P(0) = 30$ and t is the time in years. What is $\lim\limits_{t \to \infty} P(t)$?

(A) 112

(B) 224

(C) 3136

(D) 12544

Answer_____

Unauthorized copying of this page is illegal

44. Water is pumped into a tank at a rate of $1000e^{\frac{t^2}{100}}$ liters/hour. This tank has a crack and is leaking at a rate of 10 liters/hour. How much water is in the tank at time $t=10$ hours, if the tank initially contains 1000 liters?

(A) 15,527

(B) 15,427

(C) 14,527

(D) 14,427

Answer_____

45. For time $t \geq 0$ seconds, the position of an object traveling along a curve in the xy-plane is given by the parametric equations $x(t)$ and $y(t)$, where $\dfrac{dx}{dt}=t+4$ and $\dfrac{dy}{dt}=t^2+2t.$

At what time t is the speed of the object 12 units per second?

(A) 1.702

(B) 2.344

(C) 3.200

(D) 5.882

Answer_____

Unauthorized copying of this page is illegal

Examination IV

Section I Part A

Directions: Solve each of the following problems, using the space provided. Choose the best answer. Do not spend too much time on any one problem. Calculators may NOT be used on this part of the exam.

In this Exam: (1) Unless otherwise specified, the domain of a function is assumed to be the set of all real numbers x for which $f(x)$ is a real number.

(2) The inverse of a trigonometric function f may be indicated using the inverse function notation f^{-1} or with the prefix "arc" (e.g., $\sin^{-1} x = \arcsin x$)

1. $\displaystyle\int_{3}^{\infty} \frac{1}{x^2 \sqrt{x}} dx =$

(A) $\dfrac{\sqrt{3}}{3}$

(B) $\dfrac{2\sqrt{3}}{27}$

(C) $\dfrac{2\sqrt{3}}{9}$

(D) $\dfrac{2}{27}$

Answer_____

2. Let $f(x)$ be a continuous function. What is the value of $\displaystyle\int_{3}^{15} f(x)\, dx$ if it is given that

$\displaystyle\int_{1}^{5} f(3x)\, dx = 7?$

(A) $\dfrac{7}{3}$ (B) 7   (C) 14   (D) 21

Answer_____

Unauthorized copying of this page is illegal

3. $\dfrac{d}{dx}\displaystyle\int_{0}^{\frac{\pi}{4}}\left(\cos t-\sin t\right)dt$ is equal to which of the following?

$(A)\ \sqrt{2}+1$ $(B)\ \sqrt{2}$ $(C)\ \sqrt{2}-1$ $(D)\ 0$

Answer_____

4. A particle moves along the $x-$axis so that its velocity at any time $t\geq 0$ is given by $v(t)=13t^{2}-18t+15$. Which of the following is the displacement of the particle from $t=1$ to $t=3$?

$(A)\dfrac{212}{3}$

$(B)\dfrac{238}{3}$

$(C)\dfrac{248}{3}$

$(D)\dfrac{274}{3}$

Answer _____

Unauthorized copying of this page is illegal

5. Which of the following is true for the given series:

$$\sum a_n = \sum_{n=1}^{\infty}(-1)^n\left(\frac{2}{n+2}\right); \qquad \sum b_n = \sum_{n=1}^{\infty}(-1)^n\left(\frac{n^3+4}{5^n}\right)$$

(A) Both Conditionally Convergent

(B) Both Absolutely Convergent

(C) $\sum a_n$ is Conditionally Convergent, $\sum b_n$ is Absolutely Convergent

(D) $\sum a_n$ is Conditionally Convergent, $\sum b_n$ is Divergent

Answer_____

6. $\int \sin^{-1}x\, dx =$

$(A)\ x\sin^{-1}x + \sqrt{1-x^2} + C \qquad (B)\ x\sin^{-1}x - \sqrt{1-x^2} + C$

$(C)\ \frac{x^2}{2}\sin^{-1}x - \frac{\sqrt{1-x^2}}{2} + C \qquad (D)\ x\sin^{-1}x + \frac{\sqrt{x^2-1}}{2} + C$

Answer _____

Unauthorized copying of this page is illegal

Examination IV

7. Three graphs labeled *I*, *II*, and *III* are shown. One is f, one is f', one is f''. Which is which?

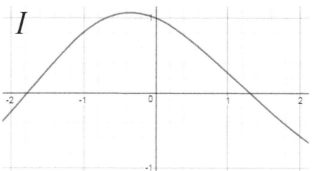

	f	f'	f''
(A)	*I*	*II*	*III*
(B)	*II*	*I*	*III*
(C)	*II*	*III*	*I*
(D)	*III*	*II*	*I*

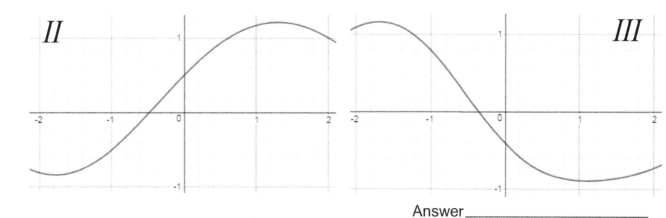

Answer_____

8. The graph of $f'(x)$ on the interval $[-1,4]$ is shown below. On what intervals is the graph of $f(x)$ concave up?

(A) $(0.5, 3.5)$

(B) $(-1, 0.5) \cup (3.5, 4)$

(C) $(2, 4)$

(D) $(0.5, 4)$

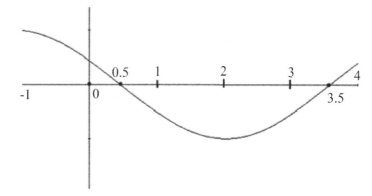

Answer _____

Unauthorized copying of this page is illegal

9. What is the radius of convergence of the Maclaurin series for $\dfrac{x}{1+x^3}$?

$(A)\,1$

$(B)\,3$

$(C)\,\dfrac{3}{2}$

$(D)\,\dfrac{1}{4}$

Answer_____

10. $\displaystyle\int_{m}^{m+h} f(x)\ dx - \int_{m}^{h} f(x)\ dx =$

$(A)\displaystyle\int_{0}^{h} f(x)\ dx$

$(B)\displaystyle\int_{h}^{h+m} f(x)\ dx$

$(C)\displaystyle\int_{h}^{m} f(x)\ dx$

$(D)\displaystyle\int_{m}^{m+h} f(x)\ dx$

Answer_____

Unauthorized copying of this page is illegal

11. Which of the following limits is equal to $\int_{1}^{3}\left(3x^2+10\right)dx$?

(A) $\lim\limits_{n\to\infty}\sum\limits_{k=1}^{n}\left(3\left(1+\dfrac{2k}{n}\right)^2+10\right)\dfrac{2}{n}$ (B) $\lim\limits_{n\to\infty}\sum\limits_{k=1}^{n}\left(3\left(\dfrac{2k}{n}\right)^2+10\right)\dfrac{2}{n}$

(C) $\lim\limits_{n\to\infty}\sum\limits_{k=1}^{n}\left(\left(\dfrac{3k}{n}\right)^2+10\right)\dfrac{3}{n}$ (D) $\lim\limits_{n\to\infty}\sum\limits_{k=1}^{n}\left(\left(1+\dfrac{3k}{n}\right)^2+10\right)\dfrac{2}{n}$

Answer_____

12. $\int\dfrac{8}{(x-2)(x-4)}\,dx=$

(A) $-4\ln|x-2|+4\ln|x-4|+C$

(B) $-2\ln|x-2|+2\ln|x-4|+C$

(C) $4\ln|x-2|-4\ln|x-4|+C$

(D) $8\ln|x-2|+8\ln|x-4|+C$

Answer_____

Unauthorized copying of this page is illegal

13. What are all values of x for which the series $\displaystyle\sum_{n=1}^{\infty} \frac{(2x-1)^n}{\sqrt[3]{n^2}}$ converge?

$(A)\ 0 < x < 1$

$(B)\ 0 \leq x < 1$

$(C)\ 0 < x \leq 1$

$(D)\ -1 \leq x < 1$

Answer_____

14. Which of the following is a power series representation for $f(x) = \dfrac{1}{4+6x}$ if $|x| < \dfrac{2}{3}$?

$(A)\ \dfrac{1}{4}\displaystyle\sum_{n=0}^{\infty}(-1)^n\left(\dfrac{3}{2}\right)^n x^n$

$(B)\ \dfrac{1}{6}\displaystyle\sum_{n=0}^{\infty}(-1)^n\left(\dfrac{2}{3}\right)^n x^n$

$(C)\ \dfrac{1}{4}\displaystyle\sum_{n=0}^{\infty}(-1)^{2n}\left(\dfrac{3}{4}\right)^n x^n$

$(D)\ \dfrac{1}{4}\displaystyle\sum_{n=0}^{\infty}\left(\dfrac{3}{2}\right)^n x^n$

Answer_____

Unauthorized copying of this page is illegal

15. Shown below is the graph of $f(x)$. Which of the following limits exist?

I. $\lim\limits_{x \to 0} f(x)$

II. $\lim\limits_{x \to 1} f(x)$

III. $\lim\limits_{x \to 2} f(x)$

(A) I only (B) I and II only (C) I and III only (D) I, II, and III

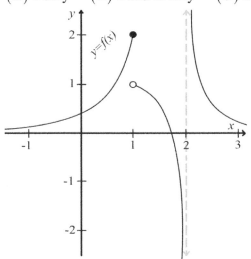

Answer_____

t	0	1	2	3	4	5
$f(t)$	0	50	90	200	275	350

16. The table above shows the total distance $f(t)$ a bicyclist has traveled along a straight road in meters during t seconds. What is approximately the velocity of the bicyclist at $t = 4$ seconds?

(A) 75 m/sec (B) 50 m/sec (C) 40 m/sec (D) 25 m/sec

Answer_____

Unauthorized copying of this page is illegal

17. What is equation of the tangent line to the graph of $y = x - e^{-x}$ that is parallel to the line $6x - 2y = 15$?

$(A)\ y = 3x + 2\ln 2 - 2$ $(B)\ y = 3x + 2\ln 2 + 2$

$(C)\ y = 3x - 2\ln 2 - 2$ $(D)\ y = 3x - 2\ln 2 + 2$

Answer_____

18. The polar curves $r = -\cos\theta$ and $r = \sqrt{3} + \cos\theta$ are shown in the figure. Which of the following expressions gives the area of the shaded region?

$(A)\ \int_{\frac{\pi}{2}}^{\pi}\left[\left(-\cos\theta\right)^2 + \left(\sqrt{3} + \cos\theta\right)^2\right]d\theta$

$(B)\ \dfrac{1}{2}\int_{\frac{\pi}{2}}^{\frac{5\pi}{6}}\left(-\cos\theta\right)^2 d\theta + \dfrac{1}{2}\int_{\frac{5\pi}{6}}^{\pi}\left(\sqrt{3} + \cos\theta\right)^2 d\theta$

$(C)\ \int_{\frac{\pi}{2}}^{\frac{5\pi}{6}}\left(\sqrt{3} + \cos\theta\right)^2 d\theta + \int_{\frac{5\pi}{6}}^{\pi}\left(-\cos\theta\right)^2 d\theta$

$(D)\ \int_{\frac{\pi}{2}}^{\frac{5\pi}{6}}\left(-\cos\theta\right)^2 d\theta + \int_{\frac{5\pi}{6}}^{\pi}\left(\sqrt{3} + \cos\theta\right)^2 d\theta$

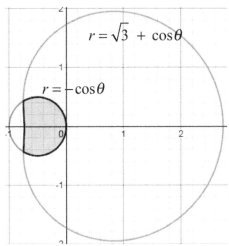

$r = \sqrt{3} + \cos\theta$

$r = -\cos\theta$

Answer_____

Unauthorized copying of this page is illegal

19. If $f(x) = \sqrt{6\sin x + 9}$, then the derivative of f at $x = 0$ is

$(A)\dfrac{1}{2\sqrt{3}}$ $(B)0$ $(C)1$ $(D)\sqrt{3}$

Answer_____

20. Which of the following statements are true regarding the series below:

$$\frac{1}{2} + \frac{(x-25)}{4} + \frac{(x-25)^2}{8} + \ldots + \frac{(x-25)^n}{2^{n+1}} + \ldots?$$

I. Interval where the series converges is $23 < x < 27$.

II. The sum of the series where it converges is equal to $\dfrac{1}{27\text{-}x}$.

III. If $x = 28$, series converges to $\dfrac{1}{3}$

IV. Interval where the series converges is $21 < x < 29$.

(A) I only (B) III only (C) I and II only (D) II and IV only

Answer _____

Unauthorized copying of this page is illegal

21. Given the equation of the curve $xy = 5 + y$, where y is the twice differentiable function of x, what is y''?

(A) $\dfrac{1-x+y}{(x-1)^2}$

(B) $\dfrac{2y}{(x-1)^2}$

(C) $-\dfrac{2y}{(x-1)^2}$

(D) $\dfrac{-y}{(x-1)}$

Answer_____

22. The graph of f', the first derivative of the function f, consists of a quarter circle of radius 5 and two line segments, as shown in the figure below. If $f(0) = -1$, what is $f(10)$?

(A) $\dfrac{25\pi}{2} + 7$ (B) $\dfrac{25\pi}{2} + 8$ (C) $\dfrac{25\pi}{4} + 7$ (D) $\dfrac{25\pi}{4}$

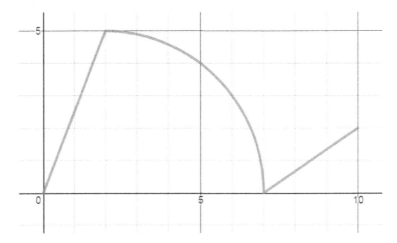

Answer_____

Unauthorized copying of this page is illegal

23. The local linear approximation to the function $h(x)$ at $x = \dfrac{1}{32}$ is $y = 32x + 16$. What is the value of $h\left(\dfrac{1}{32}\right) - h'\left(\dfrac{1}{32}\right)$?

(A) -14

(B) 1

(C) -15

(D) -1

Answer _____

24. Shown below is the graph of the differentiable function $f(x)$. Which of the following statements about $f(x)$ must be true?

I. $f'(c) = 0$ for some value c in the closed interval $[0,5]$

II. $f(c) = 0$ for some value c in the open interval $(0,5)$

III. $f'(x) < 0$ on the open interval $(0,5)$

(A) I only (B) II only (C) I and III only (D) II and III only

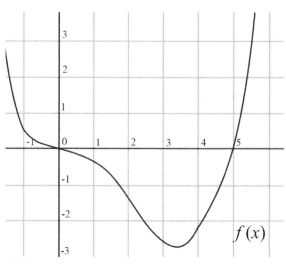

Answer _____

25. $\int \dfrac{3x^2 - 11x + 19}{x+2}\,dx =$

$(A)\,\dfrac{3}{2}x^2 - \dfrac{11}{2}x + 106\ln|x+2| + C$

$(B)\,\dfrac{3}{2}x^2 - 17x + 53\ln|x+2| + C$

$(C)\,\dfrac{x^3 - \dfrac{11}{2}x^2 + 19x}{\dfrac{x^2}{2} + 2x} + C$

$(D)\,\dfrac{(6x-11)(x+2) - (3x^2 - 11x + 19)}{(x+2)^2} + C$

Answer_____

26. A particle moves to the right along the x-axis until it reaches the origin and then moves along the x-axis to the left. The velocity of this particle is given by $v(t) = 20 - 4t$ for $t \geq 0$.

What is the position of the particle at any time t?

$(A)\,-2t^2 + 20t - 50$

$(B)\,-2t^2 + 20t + 50$

$(C)\,-4t^2 + 20t$

$(D)\,-4t^2 + 20t - 50$

Answer_____

Unauthorized copying of this page is illegal

27. Let $f(t) = \dfrac{3}{t^2}$. For what value of t is $f'(t)$ equal to the average rate of change of f on a closed interval $[a,b]$?

$(A)\sqrt[3]{\dfrac{2a^2b^2}{a-b}}$ $(B)\sqrt[3]{\dfrac{2a^2b^2}{a+b}}$ $(C)-\sqrt[3]{\dfrac{2a^2b^2}{a+b}}$ $(D)\sqrt[3]{\dfrac{a^2b^2}{a+b}}$

Answer_____

28. Shown below is the slope field of which differential equation?

$(A)\ \dfrac{dy}{dx} = xy - y$

$(B)\ \dfrac{dy}{dx} = 3y^2 - 4$

$(C)\ \dfrac{dy}{dx} = xy$

$(D)\ \dfrac{dy}{dx} = 5x$

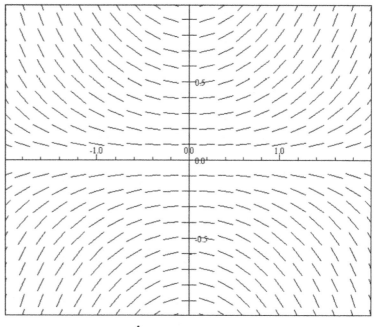

Answer_____

Unauthorized copying of this page is illegal

29. Let $y = f(x)$ be the solution to the differential equation $\dfrac{dy}{dx} = f'(x)$ with the initial condition $f(3) = 10$. Selected values of $f'(x)$ are given in the table below. What is the approximation for $f(5)$ if Euler's method is used with a step size of 1, starting at $x = 3$?

(A) 10.8 (B) 11.0 (C) 11.2 (D) 11.4

x	2	3	4	5	6
$f'(x)$	1	0.8	0.6	0.3	0.1

Answer_____

30. The graph of the function $f(x)$ is shown below. If $g(x) = \int_{x}^{1} f(t)\,dt$, what is the limit of $g'(x)$ as x approaches 4?

$(A)6$ $(B)\ 3$ $(C)\ -2$ $(D)\ -3$

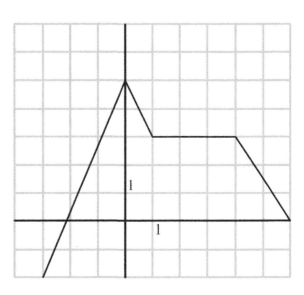

Answer _____

Unauthorized copying of this page is illegal

Examination IV

Section I Part B

Directions: Solve each of the following problems, using the space provided. Choose the best answer.
Do not spend too much time on any one problem.
A graphing calculator is required for some questions on this part of the exam.

In this Exam:

(1) The exact numerical value of the correct answer does not always appear among the choices given. Then select from among the choices the number that best approximates the exact numerical value.

(2) Unless otherwise specified, the domain of a function is assumed to be the set of all real numbers x for which $f(x)$ is a real number.

(3) The inverse of a trigonometric function f may be indicated using the inverse function notation f^{-1} or with the prefix "arc" (e.g., $\sin^{-1}x = \arcsin x$)

---

31. What approximately is the area under the curve $f(x) = x^2 + 4x + 6$ on the interval $[2,6]$ using the Right Riemann sum where P is the partition of $[2,6]$ determined by $\{2,4,5,6\}$?

(A) 193

(B) 160

(C) 195

(D) 143

Answer _____

Unauthorized copying of this page is illegal

32. The second derivative of function f is given by $f''(x) = \sin\left(e^{0.3x}\right) + \dfrac{x}{35}$. How many relative

maximum points does $f'(x)$ have in the interval $0 < x < 10$?

(A) One

(B) Two

(C) Three

(D) More than three

Answer_____

33. Given $f''(x) = 3 + 4\cos x$, $f'(0) = 0$, and $f(0) = 0$. The line, tangent to the graph of $f(x)$ and

parallel to the segment connecting the endpoints of the interval $[0,5]$, touches $f(x)$ at $x = ?$

(A) 0.596   (B) 1.018   (C) 1.381   (D) 2.073

Answer_____

Unauthorized copying of this page is illegal

34. Given differentiable function $f(x) = 2 + \int_0^{2x} \sin(t^3) dt$. Which of the following is the smallest positive number c for which $f'(c) = 0$?

(A) 0.327

(B) 0.463

(C) 0.656

(D) 0.732

Answer_____

35. Let R be the region bounded by the graphs: $y = 2x$, $y = kx$, $x = 0$, $x = 10$. If the area of R is 50, and $0 < k < 2$, the value of k is :

(A) 1.00

(B) 1.25

(C) 1.50

(D) 1.75

Answer_____

Unauthorized copying of this page is illegal

36. Which of the following series diverge?

I. $\sum_{n=1}^{\infty} \dfrac{3n^{\frac{9}{2}}(8n+1)!}{4n^6(8n)!}$ II. $\sum_{n=1}^{\infty} \dfrac{1}{n^{\frac{1}{3}}}$ III. $\sum_{n=1}^{\infty} \dfrac{1}{e^n}$

(A) I only (B) II only (C) I and II only (D) II and III only

Answer _____

37. Let $f(x)$ be a continuous and differentiable function on the interval $0 \le x \le 1$, and let $g(x) = f(2x)$. The table below gives values of $f'(x)$, the derivative of $f(x)$. What is the value of $g'(0.2)$?

(A) 2.32

(B) 3.01

(C) 4.64

(D) 6.02

x	0.1	0.2	0.3	0.4	0.5	0.6
$f'(x)$	2.05	2.32	2.56	3.01	3.52	3.75

Answer _____

Unauthorized copying of this page is illegal

38. The distance between the coastline and the flood barrier is the distance between the two curves $r = 5$ and $r = 5 - 3\sin(2\theta)$ as it changes for $0 < \theta < \dfrac{\pi}{2}$. What is the rate at which the distance between the coastline and the barrier is changing with respect to θ when $\theta = \dfrac{\pi}{6}$?

$(A)\ 6\sqrt{3}$ $(B)\ 3$ $(C)\ -3$ $(D)\ 3\sqrt{3}$

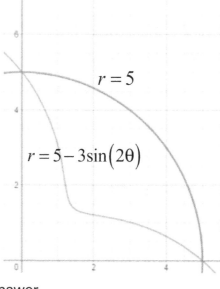

$r = 5$

$r = 5 - 3\sin(2\theta)$

Answer _____

39. Let $P_3(x)$ be a a third-degree Taylor polynomial for a function f about $x = 2$. Using information from the graph of $\left| f^{(4)}(x) \right|$ shown below, what is the maximum error in the approximation of $f(1.5)$ when you use $P_3(x)$ to approximate it?

$(A)\ 0.001$ $(B)\ 0.008$ $(B)\ 0.012$ $(B)\ 0.018$

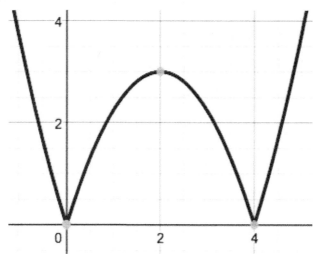

Answer _____

Unauthorized copying of this page is illegal

40. The function f has the properties indicated in the table below. Which of the following must be true?

(A) f is continuous at $x = 9$

(B) f is differentiable at $x = 8$

(C) f is continuous at $x = 8$

(D) f is continuous at $x = 7$

a	$\lim\limits_{x \to a^-} f(x)$	$\lim\limits_{x \to a^+} f(x)$	$f(a)$
7	3	3	1
8	6	6	6
9	4	5	-2

Answer_____

41. The acceleration of a particle moving along the line is given by $a(t) = t\cos(t^2)$. If at time $t = 0$ sec, its velocity is $2m/\sec$ and position is $4m$, what is the position of the particle at time $t = 7\sec$?

(A) 4.303 m

(B) 14.303 m

(C) 17.697 m

(D) 18.303 m

Answer _____

Unauthorized copying of this page is illegal

Examination IV

42. Let f be a function with $f(0) = 3$, $f'(0) = -1$, and $f''(0) = -2$. Which of the following could be the graph of the second-degree Taylor polynomial for f about $x = 0$?

(A)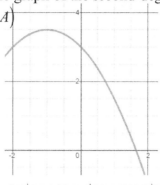

(B)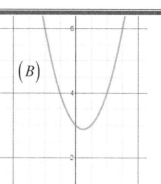

(C)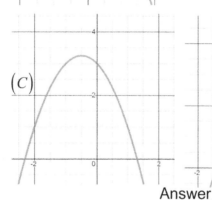

(D)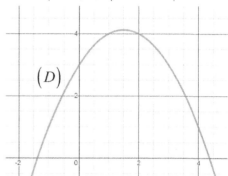

Answer_____

43. For $t \geq 0$, the position of a particle moving along the x-axis is given by $x(t) = t^5 - t^4 - 2t^3 + 3t^2 + 7t - 11$. At what time t does the velocity $v(t)$ of the particle changes from increasing to decreasing?

(A) 0   (B) 0.449   (C) 0.896   (D) 1.335

Answer _____

Unauthorized copying of this page is illegal

44. A solid has its base the region R bounded by the graph of $y = 3\sqrt{x}$, the horizontal line $y = 9$, and the y-axis. Which of the following is the integral expression that gives the volume of the solid if every cross section perpendicular to the y-axis is a rectangle whose height is 5 times the length of its base in region R?

$(A)\ 5\int_0^9 \left(3\sqrt{x}\right)^2 dx$ $(B)\ \int_0^9 \left(3\sqrt{x}\right)\left(15\sqrt{x}\right)\ dx$ $(C)\ \dfrac{5}{81}\int_0^9 y^4 dy$ $(D)\ \dfrac{5}{9}\int_0^9 y^2 dy$

Answer_____

45. If $f(x) = \int_2^{x^2} \sin t\ dt$ is continuous for all real numbers and $g(x)$ is the derivative of $f(x)$, what is $g'(5)$?

$(A)\ 9.912$ $(B)\ 49.428$ $(C)\ 98.856$ $(D)\ 110.828$

Answer_____

Unauthorized copying of this page is illegal

Examination V

Directions: Solve each of the following problems, using the space provided. Choose the best answer. Do not spend too much time on any one problem. Calculators may NOT be used on this part of the exam.

In this Exam: (1) Unless otherwise specified, the domain of a function is assumed to be the set of all real numbers x for which $f(x)$ is a real number.

(2) The inverse of a trigonometric function f may be indicated using the inverse function notation f^{-1} or with the prefix "arc" (e.g., $\sin^{-1} x = \arcsin x$)

1. Let $y = f(x)$ be a particular solution to the differential equation $\dfrac{dy}{dx} = xy^3$ with $f(1) = 2$. What is the approximate value of $f(1.1)$ if the equation of the line tangent to the graph of $y = f(x)$ at $x = 1$ is being used to approximate $f(1.1)$?

(A) 3

(B) 2.2

(C) 2.6

(D) 2.8

Answer _____

2. A function f satisfies the given conditions:

$$\lim_{x \to \infty} f(x) = 0 \qquad \lim_{x \to -\infty} f(x) = 0 \qquad \lim_{x \to 0^+} f(x) = \infty \qquad \lim_{x \to 0^-} f(x) = \infty$$

Which of the following is a possible graph for f, assuming that it does not cross a horizontal asymptote?

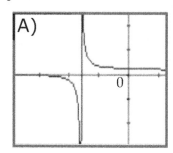

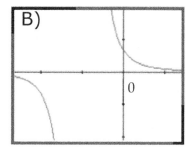

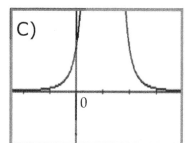

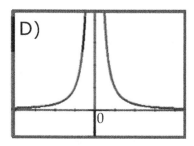

Answer _____

3. The graphs of functions f and g are shown in the figures below. Which of the following statements is true?

$(A) \lim_{x \to 0} \big(f(x)g(x+1)\big) = 2$

$(B) \lim_{x \to 0} f(x) = 1$

$(C) \lim_{x \to 0} g(x) = 2$

$(D) \lim_{x \to 0} \big(f(x+1)g(x)\big)$ does not exist

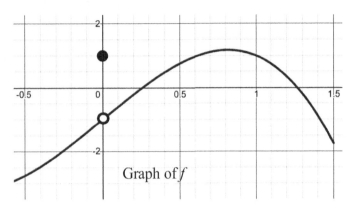

Graph of f

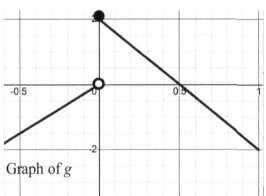

Graph of g

Answer_____

4. Which of the following is the power series representation of xe^{2x+1} ?

$(A) x - 2x^2 + (2)^2 \dfrac{x^3}{2!} - (2)^3 \dfrac{x^4}{3!} + \ldots$

$(B) x^2 + 2x^4 + (2)^2 \dfrac{x^6}{2!} + (2)^3 \dfrac{x^8}{3!} + \ldots$

$(C) ex + 2ex^2 + (2)^2 e\dfrac{x^3}{2!} + (2)^3 e\dfrac{x^4}{3!} + \ldots$

$(D) x + (2x+1)x + \dfrac{(2x+1)^2}{2!}x + \dfrac{(2x+1)^3}{3!}x + \ldots$

Answer _____

Unauthorized copying of this page is illegal

5. Which of the following series converge?

I. $\displaystyle\sum_{n=2}^{\infty} \frac{1}{n(\ln n)^4}$ II. $\displaystyle\sum_{n=1}^{\infty} \frac{3+\sin n}{n^4}$ III. $\displaystyle\sum_{n=1}^{\infty} \frac{7n^2-5}{e^n(n+3)^2}$

(A) I and II only

(B) II and III only

(C) I and III only

(D) I, II, and III

Answer_____

6. $\displaystyle\int \frac{18x-17}{(2x-3)(x+1)}dx =$

$(A)\,8\ln|2x-3|+7\ln|x+1|+C$

$(B)\,2\ln|2x-3|+7\ln|x+1|+C$

$(C)\,4\ln|2x-3|+7\ln|x+1|+C$

$(D)\,7\ln|2x-3|+2\ln|x+1|+C$

Answer_____

Unauthorized copying of this page is illegal

7. Graph of $f''(x)$, the second derivative of function $f(x)$

is shown on the right. What must be true about $f(x)$?

I. $f(x)$ is concave downward for all $a < x < b$.

II. $f(x)$ must have a critical points at $x = a$ and $x = c$.

III. The slope of $f(x)$ increases when $x < a$.

(A) I only (B) III only (C) I and III only (D) I, II and III

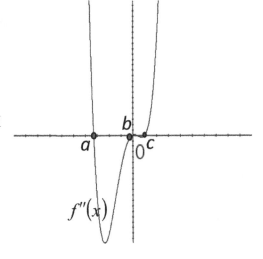

Answer_____

8. $\int e^x \cos(e^x - 2)\, dx =$

$(A)\ \sin\,(e^x - 2) + C$

$(B)\ -e^x \sin\,(e^x - 2) + C$

$(C)\ e^x \sin\,(e^x - 2x) + C$

$(D)\ \dfrac{1}{2}\sin^2\,(e^x - 2x) + C$

Answer_____

Unauthorized copying of this page is illegal

9. If $f(x) = x^3 - 6x$, which of the following are the absolute maximum and absolute minimum of $f(x)$ on the interval $[-3,2]$?

(A) Max: $f(\sqrt{2})$, Min: $f(-\sqrt{2})$　　(B) Max: $f(\sqrt{2})$, Min: $f(-3)$

(C) Max: $f(-\sqrt{2})$, Min: $f(2)$　　(D) Max: $f(-\sqrt{2})$, Min: $f(-3)$

Answer _____

10. $\displaystyle \lim_{x \to 0} \frac{e^x + 2e^{-x} - 3}{x - \sin 2x} =$

$(A) -3$

$(B) -1$

$(C) 1$

$(D) 3$

Answer _____

Unauthorized copying of this page is illegal

11. What is the area under the curve of $F(x) = f(x) - g(x)$ for $-3 \le x \le 3$ if $f(x) = 12 - g(x)$?

(A) $72 - 2 \int_{-3}^{3} g(x)dx$

(B) $72 + \int_{-3}^{3} f(x)dx$

(C) $72 + 2 \int_{-3}^{3} g(x)dx$

(D) $\int_{-3}^{3} (6 - g(x))dx$

Answer_____

12. A particle moves along a straight line. The graph below, which consists of a semicircle and a segment shows the velocity in meters per second of a particle. What is the total distance in meters traveled by the particle over the time interval from $t = 0$ sec to $t = 5$ sec?

$(A) 2\pi - 1.5$ $(B) 4\pi + 1.5$ $(C) 2\pi + 1.5$ $(D) 2\pi + \sqrt{10}$

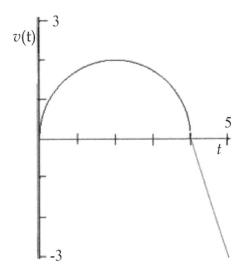

Answer_____

Unauthorized copying of this page is illegal

13. Let $P(x) = 7x + \frac{5}{2}x^2$ be the second-degree Taylor polynomial for $f(x)$ around $x = 0$. If $g(x)$ is the inverse of $f(x)$, what is $g'(0)$?

$(A)\,1 \quad (B)\,\frac{1}{5} \quad (C)\,\frac{1}{7} \quad (D)\,5$

Answer_____

14. Which of the following is a power series representation for $\ln(1 + 2x)$?

$(A)\ 2x - \frac{4x^2}{2} + \frac{8x^3}{3} - \frac{16x^4}{4} + \frac{32x^5}{5} + \ldots$

$(B)\ 2 - 4x + 8x^2 - 16x^3 + 32x^4 + \ldots$

$(C)\ 2x^2 - 4x^4 + 8x^6 - 16x^8 + 32x^{10} + \ldots$

$(D)\ 2x^2 - \frac{4x^4}{2} + \frac{8x^6}{3} - \frac{16x^8}{4} + \frac{32x^{10}}{5} + \ldots$

Answer_____

Unauthorized copying of this page is illegal

15. Let $G(x)$ be a continuous function on the closed interval $[0, 7]$. If $G(0) = -4$ and $G(7) = 5$, then the Intermediate Value Theorem guarantees that

$(A) G(3.5) = 6.5$

$(B) G'(t) = 2.3$ for at least one t between 0 and 7

$(C) G'(t) = 0$ for at least one t between 0 and 7

$(D) G(t) = 0$ for at least one t between 0 and 7

Answer _____

16. What is the interval of convergence for the power series $\sum_{n=1}^{\infty} (-1)^n \frac{n+3}{n \cdot 4^n} (x-2)^n$?

$(A) -4 < x \leq 4$

$(B) -4 < x < 4$

$(C) -2 < x \leq 6$

$(D) -2 < x < 6$

Answer _____

Unauthorized copying of this page is illegal

17. $\left(\tan^{-1}\left(e^{x^2} \right) \right)' = ?$

$(A) \dfrac{2xe^{x^2}}{1+e^{2x^2}}$ $(B) \dfrac{4xe^{x^2}}{1+e^{x^4}}$ $(C) \dfrac{2x}{1+e^{2x^2}}$ $(D) \dfrac{2xe^{x^2}}{1+e^{x^2}}$

Answer_____

18. For time $t \geq 0$, the velocity of a particle moving along the x-axis is given by $v(t) = (2t+7)^3(t-5)$. At what time t is the acceleration of the particle equal to zero?

$(A) \dfrac{23}{8}$

$(B) \dfrac{22}{9}$

$(C) 1$

$(D) \dfrac{3}{2}$

Answer_____

19. Which of the following statements about the series $\displaystyle\sum_{n=1}^{\infty}\frac{2}{3^n+\sqrt{n}}$ is true?

(A) The series converges by the nth term test.

(B) The series diverges by the limit comparison to $\displaystyle\sum_{n=1}^{\infty}\frac{1}{\sqrt{n}}$

(C) The series diverges by the nth term test.

(D) The series converges by limit comparison to the geometric series $\displaystyle\sum_{n=1}^{\infty}\frac{1}{3^n}$

Answer_____

20. $\displaystyle\int_{-8}^{1}\frac{1}{\sqrt[3]{x}}\,dx$ is

(A) $\dfrac{15}{2}$

(B) nonexistent

(C) 0

(D) $\dfrac{-9}{2}$

Answer_____

Unauthorized copying of this page is illegal

21. Which of the following is the solution to the differential equation $\dfrac{dy}{dx} = \dfrac{x-5}{y+1}$; $y \neq -1$,

subject to initial conditions $y(0) = 3$?

$(A)\, y = x - 6$

$(B)\, y = \sqrt{(x-5)^2 - 9} - 1$

$(C)\, y = \sqrt{(x-5)^2 - 9}$

$(D)\, y = \sqrt{(x-5)^2 - 16}$

Answer_____

22. If $\displaystyle\int_{60}^{150} v(t)\,dt = 127$, and $\displaystyle\int_{80}^{150} v(t)\,dt = -78$, what is $\displaystyle\int_{60}^{80} v(t)\,dt$?

$(A)\ 49$ $(B)\ 205$ $(C)\ -205$ $(D)\ -49$

Answer_____

23. At time t, the number of bacteria grows at the rate of $3e^{1.5t} + 8t$ bacteria per hour, where t is measured in days. By how much has the number of bacteria grown from time $t = 0$ days to $t = 20$ days?

$(A)\ 4.5e^{30} + 3198$

$(B)\ 3e^{30} + 1598$

$(C)\ 2e^{30} + 1600$

$(D)\ 2e^{30} + 1598$

Answer _____

24. Which of the following integrals represents the length of the curve of $f(x) = \ln(\sec x)$ between $x = 0$ and $x = \dfrac{\pi}{4}$?

$(A)\ \displaystyle\int_0^{\frac{\pi}{4}} \sqrt{1 + \tan^2 x}\ dx$

$(B)\ \displaystyle\int_0^{\frac{\pi}{4}} \left(1 + \sec^2 x\right) dx$

$(C)\ \displaystyle\int_0^{\frac{\pi}{4}} \sqrt{1 + \cos^2 x}\ dx$

$(D)\ \displaystyle\int_0^{\frac{\pi}{4}} \sqrt{1 + \left(\ln(\sec x)\right)^2}\ dx$

Answer _____

Unauthorized copying of this page is illegal

Examination V

25. Shown below is the slope field for which differential equation?

(A) $\dfrac{dy}{dx} = 1 + y^2$

(B) $\dfrac{dy}{dx} = x - y$

(C) $\dfrac{dy}{dx} = 1 + x^2$

(D) $\dfrac{dy}{dx} = 1 - y^2 + x^2$

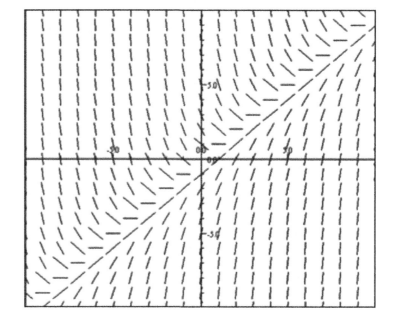

Answer_____

26. An electron travels along the path defined by the polar equation $r = 4 - 3\cos\theta$ and has the position $(x(t), y(t))$ at time t. Given that $\dfrac{d^2y}{d\theta^2} = \dfrac{dy}{dt}$ and $\theta = 0$ when $t = 0$, what is $\dfrac{dy}{dt}$ at $\theta = \dfrac{\pi}{4}$?

(A) $-6 - 2\sqrt{2}$ (B) $\dfrac{3\sqrt{2}}{2}$ (C) $6 - 2\sqrt{2}$ (D) $6 + 2\sqrt{2}$

Answer _____

Unauthorized copying of this page is illegal

27. Let f be a function that is differentiable on $(0,15)$. If $f(1)=5$, $f(6)=-3$, $f(11)=5$, which of the following must be true?

I. For some c, $1 < c < 6$, $f(c) = -4$

II. The graph of f has at least one horizontal tangent

III. f has at least 3 zeros

(A) *I* only

(B) *I* and *II* only

(C) *II* only

(D) *II* and *III* only

Answer_____

28. The length of a curve $y = f(x)$ from $x = a$ to $x = b$ is given by $\int_{a}^{b} \sqrt{9x^2 + 12x + 5}\ dx$. Which of the following could $f(x)$ be equal to?

(A) $3x + 2$ $\quad(B)$ $\dfrac{3x^2}{2} + 5x + C$ $\quad(C)$ $\dfrac{3x^2}{2} + 2x + C$ $\quad(D)$ $3x^3 + 6x^2 + 5x + C$

Answer_____

Unauthorized copying of this page is illegal

Examination V

29. The temperature of a liquid at time $t \geq 0$ is modeled by the nonconstant function P and changes according to the differential equation $\dfrac{dP}{dt} = \dfrac{1}{8}P + 3$, where $P(t)$ is measured in degrees Fahrenheit and t is measured in minutes. Which of the following must be true?

$(A)\ \ln\left|\dfrac{1}{8}P + 3\right| = 8t + C$

$(B)\ P = e^{\frac{1}{8}P+3} + C$

$(C)\ \ln\left|\dfrac{1}{8}P + 3\right| = \dfrac{1}{8}t + C$

$(D)\ P = \dfrac{1}{16}P^2 + 3t + C$

Answer_____

30. The coefficient of $(x-3)^2$ in the Taylor series for $f(x) = \arctan x$ about $x = 3$ is:

$(A)\ \dfrac{3}{100}$ $\qquad$ $(B)\ -\dfrac{3}{100}$ $\qquad$ $(C)\ -\dfrac{3}{50}$ $\qquad$ $(D)\ \dfrac{3}{50}$

Answer_____

Unauthorized copying of this page is illegal

Examination V

Directions: Solve each of the following problems, using the space provided. Choose the best answer.
Do not spend too much time on any one problem.
A graphing calculator is required for some questions on this part of the exam.

In this Exam:

(1) The exact numerical value of the correct answer does not always appear among the choices given.
Then select from among the choices the number that best approximates the exact numerical value.

(2) Unless otherwise specified, the domain of a function is assumed to be the set of all real numbers
x for which $f(x)$ is a real number.

(3) The inverse of a trigonometric function f may be indicated using the inverse function notation
f^{-1} or with the prefix "arc" (e.g., $\sin^{-1} x = \arcsin x$)

---

31. For the curve given parametrically by $x = \sin(5t), y = \cos(5t)$, where $2.4 \le t \le 3$, what is the
point on the curve at which the tangent line to this curve is vertical?

(A) $\left(\dfrac{\sqrt{2}}{2}, 0 \right)$ (B) $(1, 0)$ (C) $(1, 1)$ (D) $\left(\dfrac{1}{2}, 0 \right)$

Answer _____

Unauthorized copying of this page is illegal

Examination V

32. While on a road trip, a girl drives for 8 hours. Her velocity, recorded at random times in miles per hour, is given in the table below. Using a trapezoidal sum with the 4 subintervals indicated by the table, how many miles has she driven after 8 hours?

(A) 320 miles (B) 325 miles (C) 328 miles (D) 330 miles

t	0	1	5	6	8
$v(t)$	25	30	60	45	20

Answer_____

33. At 3:00 PM car A is 50 miles south of car B and is driving north at a rate of 25mph. If car B is driving west at a rate of 15 mph, at what time is the distance between the cars minimal?

(A) 4:12 PM (B) 4:28 PM (C) 4:45 PM (D) 3:44 PM

Answer_____

Unauthorized copying of this page is illegal

34. The first derivative of the function f is defined by $f'(x) = (x^2 - 4x + 6)\sin(x - 3)$ for $0 < x < 6$. On which of the following intervals is the graph of f concave down?

(A) $(0,3)$

(B) $(0, 0.821)$ and $(5.064, 6)$

(C) $(0, 1.081)$ and $(5.064, 6)$

(D) $(0, 0.821)$

Answer_____

35. The number of a certain bacteria doubles every 15 sec. Its rate of growth is directly proportional to the number of bacteria present. If the initial number of bacteria is 75,000, what is the number of bacteria after 15 min?

(A) 6.485×10^{27} (B) 9.067×10^{28} (C) 8.647×10^{22} (D) 6.452×10^{15}

Answer_____

Unauthorized copying of this page is illegal

36. Cream puffs are being filled with custard at the rate $r(t) = 80t^{\frac{1}{4}}$ cream puffs per minute, with $t \geq 0$ measured in minutes. If there were 700 filled cream puffs to begin with, how many cream puffs are filled after 625 minutes?

$(A)100700$ $(B)200000$ $(C)200700$ $(D)300000$

Answer_____

37. Let $f(t) = \arcsin(t)$ for $0 \leq t \leq 1$. For what value of t is the instantaneous rate of change of $f(t)$ equal to the average rate of change of $f(t)$ on the closed interval $[0.5, 1]$?

$(A)\ 0.4726$ $(B)\ 0.8787$ $(C)\ 0.6868$ $(D)\ 0.9435$

Answer _____

38. What is the length of curve given parametrically: $x = \sin(t^2)$, $y = 2\cos(\ln t)$, $\dfrac{\pi}{2} < t < \dfrac{3\pi}{2}$?

(A) 1.947

(B) 6.351

(C) 12.499

(D) 13.063

Answer_____

39. Cans are being brought to a recycling plant at a rate modeled by $R(t) = 20\left(\dfrac{t}{200}\right)^2\left(1 - \dfrac{t}{400}\right)^3$

for $0 \le t \le 200$ where $R(t)$ is measured in tons per day and t is measured in days.

While cans are entering the plant, they are being taken from it to the processing center at a constant rate of 1 tons of cans per day. At time $t = 0$, there are 60 tons of cans at the recycling plant. How many tons of cans are there at the recycling plant at $t = 200$?

(A) 60 (B) 150 (C) 210 (D) 410

Answer _____

Unauthorized copying of this page is illegal

40. Consider the area of the region bounded by the graph of $y = \left(x - \dfrac{1}{2}\right)^2 + \dfrac{1}{2}$ and the x-axis in

the interval $\left[0,2\right]$. Arrange the following in increasing order:

(I) Area calculated using Right Riemann Sums with four subintervals

(II) Area calculated using Left Riemann Sums with four subintervals

(III) Area calculated by evaluating the integral.

$(A)\, I,\, III,\, II$

$(B)\, I,\, II,\, III$

$(C)\, II,\, I,\, III$

$(D)\, II,\, III,\, I$

Answer_____

41. The position $r(t)$ of a particle at time t is given by the vector $\left(3\cos(4t), -\sin^2 t\right)$. What is the

particle's velocity at $t = 3$?

$(A)(6.439, 0.279)$ $(B)(6.439, -0.279)$ $(C)(-1.609, 0.279)$ $(D)(-6.439, -0.279)$

Answer_____

Unauthorized copying of this page is illegal

42. The base of a container is defined by the region bounded by the graph of $y = -x^2 + 6x + 9$ in the first quadrant. The cross-sections of the container are semicircles perpendicular to the x-axis. Which of the following represents the volume of the container?

$(A)\ 2\pi \displaystyle\int_{0}^{7.24264} \left(\frac{1}{2}(-x^2 + 6x + 9) \right)^2 dx$

$(B)\ \dfrac{\pi}{2} \displaystyle\int_{0}^{7.24264} \left(\frac{1}{2}(-x^2 + 6x + 9) \right)^2 dx$

$(C)\ \pi \displaystyle\int_{0}^{7.24264} \left(\frac{1}{2}(-x^2 + 6x + 9) \right)^2 dx$

$(D)\ \dfrac{1}{2} \displaystyle\int_{-1.24264}^{7.24264} \left(-x^2 + 6x + 9 \right)^2 dx$

Answer_____

43. The function f is differentiable on the closed interval $[-2, 6]$ and satisfies $f(0) = -1$. The graph of f', the derivative of f, consists of a semicircle and three line segments, as shown in the figure below. What is the absolute maximum value of f on the interval $[-2, 6]$?

$(A)\ 5 + \dfrac{\pi}{2}$ $(B)\ 6 + \dfrac{\pi}{2}$ $(C)\ 3$ $(D)\ 6 + \pi$

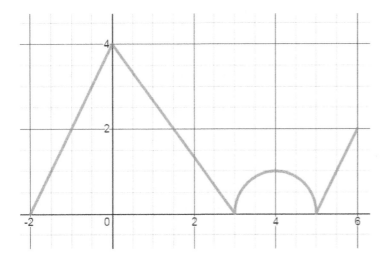

Answer_____

Unauthorized copying of this page is illegal

x	-1	2	4	6	7
f (x)	3	5	7	8	10
f'(x)	2	6	9	7	5

44. Let $g(x)$ be the inverse of $f(x)$. Given the following values on the table above, at which value $x = a$ will $g'(a) = \dfrac{1}{6}$?

$(A) -1$

$(B)\ 2$

$(C)\ 3$

$(D)\ 5$

Answer_____

45. The amount y of a radioactive substance decays according to the equation $\dfrac{dy}{dt} = ky$ where k is a constant and time, t, is measured in days. If half of the amount present will decay in 13 days, what is the value of k?

$(A) -0.053$

$(B) -0.015$

$(C)\ 0.053$

$(D)\ 0.015$

Answer_____

Examination VI

Directions: Solve each of the following problems, using the space provided. Choose the best answer. Do not spend too much time on any one problem. Calculators may NOT be used on this part of the exam.

In this Exam: (1) Unless otherwise specified, the domain of a function is assumed to be the set of all real numbers x for which $f(x)$ is a real number.

(2) The inverse of a trigonometric function f may be indicated using the inverse function notation f^{-1} or with the prefix "arc" (e.g., $\sin^{-1} x = \arcsin x$)

1. $\lim\limits_{x \to 0} \dfrac{\sin x + 2x}{4x}$ is

$(A)\ \dfrac{1}{2}$

$(B)\ \dfrac{3}{4}$

$(C)\ \dfrac{3}{8}$

(D) Nonexistent

Answer _____

2. Which of the following is the second derivative of the function described by the pair of parametric equations $x = \sin t$ and $y = \cos t$?

$(A) \sec^3 t \quad (B) -\sec^3 t \quad (C) -\dfrac{\sec^2 t}{\sin t} \quad (D) -\sec^2 t$

Answer _____

3. If $f(x) = e^e$, which of the following is $f'(x)$?

(A) e^e

(B) 0

(C) e

(D) e^{e-1}

Answer_____

4. The curves $f(x), f'(x),$ and $f''(x)$ are shown. A function $f(x)$ is increasing and concave down. What are the correct labels for graphs I, II, and III?

	I	II	III
(A)	$f'(x)$	$f(x)$	$f''(x)$
(B)	$f''(x)$	$f'(x)$	$f(x)$
(C)	$f(x)$	$f''(x)$	$f'(x)$
(D)	$f(x)$	$f'(x)$	$f''(x)$

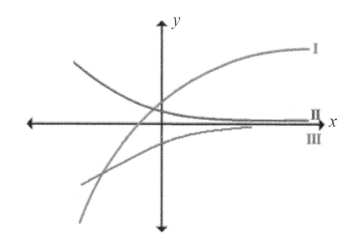

Answer_____

Unauthorized copying of this page is illegal

5. Given the function $f(x) = x^2 + 4x - 1$, for which of the following values of c on the open interval $(0,5)$ will the conclusion of the Mean Value theorem be satisfied for the function $f(x)$?

(A) $\dfrac{9}{2}$

(B) 4

(C) $\dfrac{5}{2}$

(D) $\dfrac{1}{3}$

Answer_____

6. $\lim\limits_{x \to 2} \left(f(x) \cdot g(x) \right)$ is

$(A)0$ $(B)1$ $(C)2$ (D)nonexistent

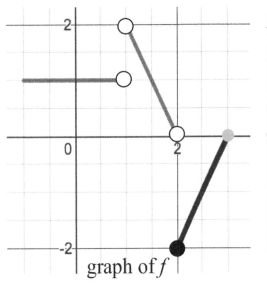

graph of f

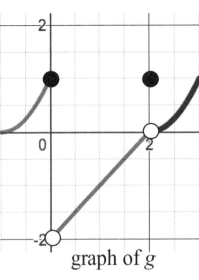

graph of g

Answer_____

Unauthorized copying of this page is illegal

7. $\int \dfrac{x^2-2}{x^3-6x+1}dx =$

(A) $\ln\left|x^3-6x+1\right|+C$

(B) $\dfrac{1}{3}\ln\left|x^3-6x+1\right|+C$

(C) $\dfrac{1}{3}\left(x^3-6x+1\right)+C$

(D) $\dfrac{\left(x^3-6x+1\right)^2}{2}+C$

Answer_____

8. What is the area of the region under the graph of $f(x)=\dfrac{1}{(x+1)(4-x)}$ from $x=0$ to $x=3$?

(A) $\dfrac{2\ln4}{5}$ (B) $\dfrac{4\ln4}{5}$ (C) $\dfrac{6\ln4}{5}$ (D) $\dfrac{8\ln4}{5}$

Answer_____

Unauthorized copying of this page is illegal

9. Let $\dfrac{dy}{dx} = e^{x-y}$. Which of the following is the solution to this equation such that $y(0) = 1$?

$(A)\, y = \ln x$

$(B)\, y = \ln(e^x + e)$

$(C)\, y = e^x$

$(D)\, y = \ln(e^x + e - 1)$

Answer _____

10. Given the function $g(x) = \begin{cases} 2 & \text{if } x \le -2 \\ -\dfrac{1}{2}x + 1 & \text{if } x > -2 \end{cases}$ what is the value of $\displaystyle\int_{-5}^{4} g(x)\,dx$?

$(A)\, 9$

$(B)\, 11$

$(C)\, 13$

$(D)\, 15$

Answer _____

Unauthorized copying of this page is illegal

11. What is y'' if $\sin y = y + 5x$?

$(A)\ \dfrac{5}{-1+\cos y}$ $(B)\dfrac{5\sin y}{\left(-1+\cos y\right)^2}$ $(C)-\dfrac{25\cos y}{\left(1+\cos y\right)^2}$ $(D)\dfrac{25\sin y}{\left(-1+\cos y\right)^3}$

Answer_____

12. What is the area of the region R enclosed by the graphs of $y = \ln\left(x^2\right), x = 1$ and $x = 3$?

$(A)\ 6\ln 3 - 4$ $(B)\ 3\ln 3 - 2$ $(C)\ 3\ln 3 + 2$ $(D)\ 3\ln 3 - 3$

Answer_____

Unauthorized copying of this page is illegal

13. Which of the following is the power series representation for the function $f(x) = \dfrac{3}{(1+x)^2}$

if $|x| < 1$?

(A) $3 - 3x + 3x^2 - 3x^3 + \ldots$

(B) $1 - x + x^2 - x^3 + \ldots$

(C) $3 - 3(2x) + 3(3x^2) - 3(4x^3) + \ldots$

(D) $1 - 2x + 3x^2 - 4x^3 + \ldots$

Answer_____

14. A curve is given parametrically by $x = \ln t, y = e^t$. What is the equation of the line tangent to the curve at $t = 12$?

(A) $y - e = 12e^{12}\left(x - e^{12}\right)$

(B) $y - e^{12} = 12e^{12}\left(x - \ln 12\right)$

(C) $y + e^{12} = -12e^{12}\left(x + \ln 12\right)$

(D) $y - e^{12} = e^{12}\left(x - \ln 12\right)$

Answer_____

Unauthorized copying of this page is illegal

15. Which of the following series converge?

I. $\sum_{n=2}^{\infty} \frac{1}{n^2 \cdot \ln n}$ II. $\sum_{n=2}^{\infty} \frac{1}{n \cdot \ln n}$ III. $\sum_{n=2}^{\infty} \frac{1}{\sqrt{n} \cdot \ln n}$

(A) I only

(B) II only

(C) I and II only

(D) I, II, and III

Answer_____

16. The position $s(t)$ of a particle on the x-axis at time t, $t \geq 0$, is $\cos t$. The average velocity of the particle for $0 \leq t \leq \pi$ is

$(A) -\frac{1}{\pi}$ $(B) \frac{2}{\pi}$ $(C) -\frac{2}{\pi}$ $(D) \frac{1}{\pi}$

Answer_____

Unauthorized copying of this page is illegal

x	0	4	6	8	16
$g(x)$	28	27	24	19	12
$g'(x)$	0	-1	-2	-3	-4

17. Let $g(x)$ be a differentiable function defined on the interval $0 \le x \le 16$. Some values of $g(x)$ and its derivative $g'(x)$ are given in the table above. Which of the following is the x - intercept of the line tangent to the graph of $g(x)$ and parallel to the segment connecting the endpoints of $g(x)$?

(A) $(23,0)$

(B) $(31,0)$

(C) $(-23,0)$

(D) $(-31,0)$

Answer_____

18. $\lim\limits_{x \to 0} \dfrac{\displaystyle\int_{2}^{2+x} \dfrac{\sin t}{3t+2}}{x} =$

$(A)\dfrac{\cos 2}{2}$ $(B)\dfrac{\sin 2}{4}$ $(C)\dfrac{\sin 2}{8}$ $(D)\dfrac{\sin(2+x)}{x(3x+2)}$

Answer _____

Unauthorized copying of this page is illegal

Examination VI

19. Which of the following is the power series representation for $f(x) = x \cdot (\text{Arc} \tan x)$ if $|x| < 1$?

(A) $1 - x + \dfrac{x^3}{3} - \dfrac{x^5}{5} + \dfrac{x^7}{7} - \dfrac{x^9}{9} + \ldots$

(B) $1 + x + \dfrac{x^3}{3} + \dfrac{x^5}{5} + \dfrac{x^7}{7} + \dfrac{x^9}{9} + \dfrac{x^{11}}{11} + \ldots$

(C) $x^2 - \dfrac{x^4}{3} + \dfrac{x^6}{5} - \dfrac{x^8}{7} + \dfrac{x^{10}}{9} + \ldots$

(D) $x - \dfrac{x^3}{3} + \dfrac{x^5}{5} - \dfrac{x^7}{7} + \dfrac{x^9}{9} + \ldots$

Answer_____

20. $\dfrac{d}{dx} \displaystyle\int_0^{x^3} \sqrt{t^2 + 2}\, dt =$

(A) $\sqrt{x^6 \cdot 3x^2 + 2} - \sqrt{2}$

(B) $\sqrt{x^6 + 2}$

(C) $\left(\sqrt{x^6 + 2}\right) \cdot 3x^2$

(D) $\left(\sqrt{x^6 + 2}\right) \cdot x^3$

Answer_____

Unauthorized copying of this page is illegal

21. If the length of a curve $y = f(x)$ from $x = a$ to $x = b$ is given by $L = \int\limits_a^b \sqrt{x^2 + 2x + 2}\ dx$ then $f(x)$ could be

(A) $\dfrac{x^2}{2} + 2x$

(B) $(x+1)^2$

(C) $\dfrac{x^2}{2} + x + 3$

(D) $\dfrac{x^2}{2} + 3x + 2$

Answer_____

22. Given f is continuous for all real numbers, $\dfrac{dy}{dx} = f(x)$ and $y(-1) = 6$, what is $y(x)$?

(A) $6 + \int\limits_{-1}^{x} f(t)\,dt$

(B) $\int\limits_{-1}^{x} f(t)\,dt - 6$

(C) $6 + \int\limits_{-1}^{x} f'(t)\,dt$

(D) $6 - \int\limits_{-1}^{x} f'(t)\,dt$

Answer_____

Unauthorized copying of this page is illegal

23. If f is a twice-differential function, where $\lim\limits_{x\to\infty} f(x) = 12$ and $f(6) = 5.5$,then $\int_{6}^{\infty} f'(x)\ dx$ is

$(A)\,6.5$ $(B)\,-6.5$ $(C)\,17.5$ (D) nonexistent

Answer_____

24. A spherical balloon is being filled with air. The radius increases at a rate of 1 inch per second. What is the instantaneous rate of change in volume when the radius of the balloon is 8 inches?

$(A)\,36\pi$

$(B)\,64\pi$

$(C)\,72\pi$

$(D)\,256\pi$

Answer_____

Unauthorized copying of this page is illegal

25. The region in the first quadrant bounded by the graphs of the equations $y = x^2$ and $y = 2x^2 - 4$ is revolved around the $y-$axis. What is the volume of the solid of revolution?

(A) 2π $\qquad$ (B) 3π $\qquad$ (C) 4π $\qquad$ (D) 5π

Answer_____

26. A line perpendicular to the tangent line to the curve at the point of tangency is called a normal line to the curve at that point. Which of the following is an equation of the normal line to the graph of $y = \dfrac{1 - \cos x}{1 + \cos x}$ at the point $P\left(\dfrac{\pi}{2}, 1\right)$?

(A) $y - 1 = -\dfrac{1}{2}\left(x - \dfrac{\pi}{2}\right)$

(B) $y - 1 = 2\left(x - \dfrac{\pi}{2}\right)$

(C) $y - 1 = \dfrac{1}{2}\left(x - \dfrac{\pi}{2}\right)$

(D) $y - 1 = -2\left(x - \dfrac{\pi}{2}\right)$

Answer_____

Unauthorized copying of this page is illegal

27. $\lim\limits_{h \to 0} \dfrac{4\cos^4(x+h) + 3\sin(x+h) - 4\cos^4 x - 3\sin x}{h}$ is

$(A)\,0$

$(B)\,16\cos^3 x \sin x + 3\cos x$

$(C)\,-16\cos^3 x + 3\cos x$

$(D)\,-16\cos^3 x \sin x + 3\cos x$

Answer _____

28. Which of the following is equal to $\displaystyle\int \dfrac{5}{x^2 + 6x + 10}\,dx$?

$(A)\,5\ln\left|x^2 + 6x + 10\right| + C$

$(B)\,\dfrac{5}{x+3}\tan^{-1}\dfrac{1}{x+3} + C$

$(C)\,5\tan^{-1}(x+3) + C$

$(D)\,5\tan^{-1}(x^2 + 6x + 10) + C$

Answer _____

Unauthorized copying of this page is illegal

29. A particle moving along the polar curve given by $r = 2 + 2\sin\theta$ has position $\big(x(t), y(t)\big)$ at time t, with $\theta = 0$ when $t = 0$. This particle moves along the curve so that $\dfrac{dr}{dt} = \dfrac{dr}{d\theta}$. What is the value of $\dfrac{dr}{dt}$ at $\theta = \dfrac{\pi}{6}$?

$(A)\sqrt{3}$ $(B)\dfrac{1}{2}$ $(C)\dfrac{\sqrt{3}}{2}$ $(D)\,1$

Answer＿＿＿＿＿＿＿＿＿＿

30. Two ants are moving along the curves in the xy-plane. For time $t \geq 0$, the position of ant A is given by $x = 2t - 4$ and $y = (2t - 4)^2$, and the position of ant B is given by $x = \dfrac{4t}{3} - 2$ and $y = \dfrac{4t}{3}$. What is the the exact time t at which the two ants meet each other?

$(A)\ t = 2$ $(B)\ t = \dfrac{4}{3}$ $(C)\ t = 3$ $(D)\,t = \dfrac{5}{3}$

Answer＿＿＿＿＿＿＿＿＿＿

Unauthorized copying of this page is illegal

Examination VI

Section I Part B

Directions: Solve each of the following problems, using the space provided. Choose the best answer. Do not spend too much time on any one problem.

A graphing calculator is required for some questions on this part of the exam.

In this Exam:

(1) The exact numerical value of the correct answer does not always appear among the choices given. Then select from among the choices the number that best approximates the exact numerical value.

(2) Unless otherwise specified, the domain of a function is assumed to be the set of all real numbers x for which $f(x)$ is a real number.

(3) The inverse of a trigonometric function f may be indicated using the inverse function notation f^{-1} or with the prefix "arc" (e.g., $\sin^{-1} x = \arcsin x$)

---

31. $f(0.6)$ is approximated by the fifth degree Taylor polynomial $(x-1) - \dfrac{(x-1)^3}{3!} - \dfrac{(x-1)^5}{5!}$.

Given that $\left| f^{(7)}(x) \right| \le 2$ for all x in the interval $[0.6, 1]$, what is the maximum error of $f(0.6)$?

$(A)\ 6.89 \times 10^{-7}$ $(B)\ 6.89 \times 10^{-8}$ $(C)\ 6.50 \times 10^{-7}$ $(D)\ 6.50 \times 10^{-8}$

Answer _____

Unauthorized copying of this page is illegal

32. Water leaks from a pipe into a bucket at a rate of $1.7 + \dfrac{4.5}{x}$, x being the time in minutes that the pipe has been leaking. If there is 16.52 mL of water in the bucket after 2 minutes, how much water is in the bucket after 5 minutes?

(A) 25.74 mL $\qquad$ (B) 24.67 mL $\qquad$ (C) 20.12 mL $\qquad$ (D) 16.70 mL

Answer_____

33. A cannonball is fired from the point considered to be the origin. The path of the cannonball follows the parametric equations: $y = 16\sqrt{2}t - 16t^2$ and $x = 16\sqrt{2}t$, where y is the height of the cannonball and x is the x coordinate of the cannonball. What is the total distance traveled by the cannonball from its starting point to the point at which it hits the ground again?

(A) 36.729

(B) 23.910

(C) 13.337

(D) 44.602

Answer_____

Unauthorized copying of this page is illegal

34. The function $f(x) = \left| \sin^2 x - \cos x \sin\left(\dfrac{\pi x}{2}\right) \right|$ is given on the interval $(0,5)$. Approximately at which x-coordinates is f not differentiable?

$(A) \{0.9,\ 2.4,\ 3.7\}$ $(B)\ \{0.4,\ 1.7,\ 3.1,\ 4.5\}$ $(C)\ \{2.4,\ 4.5\}$ $(D)\ \{0.9,\ 1.7,\ 4.5\}$

Answer_____

35. Let f be the function defined by $f(x) = \begin{cases} \sqrt{x+2} & \text{for } 0 \le x \le 2 \\ 4-x & \text{for } 2 < x \le 5.5 \end{cases}$

What is the average value of $f(x)$ on the closed interval $0 \le x \le 5.5$?

$(A)\ 0.786$ $(B)\ 0.891$ $(C)\ 1.043$ $(D)\ 0.915$

Answer_____

Unauthorized copying of this page is illegal

36. The graph of the function $f(x) = 4\cos x$ crosses the y-axis at point P $(0,4)$ and the x-axis at

the point Q $\left(\dfrac{\pi}{2}, 0\right)$. Which of the following is the x-coordinate of the point on the graph of $f(x)$,

between P and Q at which the line tangent to the graph of $f(x)$ is parallel to the segment

connecting points P and Q?

(A) 0.6901

(B) 0.8901

(C) 1.0601

(D) 0.1348

Answer_____

37. What is the area in the first quadrant of the region R, bounded by the y-axis, horizontal

line $y = 2$ and $y = \sqrt{x^3 + 1}$?

(A) 0.7587 (B) 1.0262 (C) 1.4423 (D) 3.2450

Answer_____

Unauthorized copying of this page is illegal

38. The temperature of a cup of tea is modeled by function H for $0 \le t \le 15$. Values of $H(t)$ for selected values of t are shown in the table below. Using a trapezoidal sum with the 5 subintervals indicated by the table, what is the approximate average temperature of the tea over 15 minutes.

(A) 53.333 °C

(B) 55.833 °C

(C) 58.333 °C

(D) 59.833 °C

Answer_____

39. The number of nonzero terms of the Taylor series for $f(x) = \cos x$ about $x = 0$ that should

be summed up to approximate $\cos \dfrac{3\pi}{180}$ to within 0.00001 is:

(A) 2

(B) 3

(C) 4

(D) 5

Answer _____

40. Which of the following tests prove that the series $\sum\limits_{n=1}^{\infty} \dfrac{n^2}{\sqrt{n^3-2n}}$ diverges?

I. Nth term test   II. Limit Comparison Test with $\sum\limits_{n=1}^{\infty} \dfrac{1}{n^{\frac{3}{2}}}$ III. Limit Comparison Test with $\sum\limits_{n=1}^{\infty} \dfrac{1}{n}$

(A) I only (B) III only (C) I and III only (D) I, II, and III

Answer_____

41. The population $P(t)$ of a species satisfies the logistic differential equation $\dfrac{dP}{dt} = P\left(70 - \dfrac{P}{80}\right)$

where the initial population $P(0) = 30$ and t is the time in years. For what value of P is the population growing the fastest?

(A) 2000

(B) 2800

(C) 4200

(D) 5600

Answer_____

Unauthorized copying of this page is illegal

42. If the function g is defined by $g(x) = \int_0^{x^2} \cos t \, dt$ on the closed interval $-\frac{1}{2} \leq x \leq \frac{5}{2}$, then g has a local maximum at $x =$

(A) 0

(B) 0.808

(C) 1.253

(D) 2.171

Answer_____

43. At any time t $\geq$ 0, in days, the rate of a mosquito population is given by $y' = ky$, where k is a constant of proportionality and y is the number of mosquitoes present. The initial population is 3,000 and the population quadruples during the first 7 days. By what factor will the population have increased in the first 14 days?

(A) 4

(B) 8

(C) 16

(D) 32

Answer _____

44. Let R be the region enclosed by $y = 3\ln x$, $x = 5$ and x – axis. What is the volume of the solid generated by revolving the region R about the x-axis?

(A) 137.330

(B) 149.532

(C) 187.913

(D) 193.879

Answer _____

45. A particle moves along the x-axis such that its acceleration from time $t = 0$ to time $t = 5$ is given by $a(t) = -2\sin(t)$. The particle has a velocity of 1 at time $t = 0$. What is the total distance traveled by the particle over the time interval?

(A) 3.288 (B) 6.918 (C) 7.640 (D) 8.288

Answer _____

Formulas and Theorems

Limits

If $\lim\limits_{x\to c} f(x)$ and $\lim\limits_{x\to c} g(x)$ both exist, then (I) – (V) are true:

$\lim\limits_{x\to c}\left[f(x)+g(x)\right]=\lim\limits_{x\to c} f(x)+\lim\limits_{x\to c} g(x)$	(I)	$\lim\limits_{x\to c}\left[af(x)\right]=a\lim\limits_{x\to c} f(x)$		(II)

$$\lim\limits_{x\to c}\left[f(x)\cdot g(x)\right]=\lim\limits_{x\to c} f(x)\cdot\lim\limits_{x\to c} g(x) \quad\text{(III)}$$

$$\lim\limits_{x\to c}\left[f(x)^{\frac{a}{b}}\right]=\left[\lim\limits_{x\to c} f(x)\right]^{\frac{a}{b}} \quad\text{(IV)}$$

$$\lim\limits_{x\to c}\left[\frac{f(x)}{g(x)}\right]=\frac{\lim\limits_{x\to c} f(x)}{\lim\limits_{x\to c} g(x)}\ \text{if}\ \lim\limits_{x\to a} g(x)\neq 0 \quad\text{(V)}$$

$$\lim\limits_{n\to 0}(1+n)^{\frac{1}{n}}=\lim\limits_{n\to\infty}\left(1+\frac{1}{n}\right)^{n}=e$$

$$\lim\limits_{x\to 0}\frac{\sin x}{x}=\lim\limits_{x\to 0}\frac{x}{\sin x}=1$$

$$\lim\limits_{x\to 0}\frac{1-\cos x}{x}=0$$

Differentiation formulas

Power Rule: $\left(x^{n}\right)'=nx^{n-1}$	Product Rule: $\left(f(x)\cdot g(x)\right)'=f'(x)\cdot g(x)+g'(x)\cdot f(x)$
Reciprocal Rule: $\left(\dfrac{1}{g(x)}\right)'=-\dfrac{g'(x)}{g^{2}(x)}$	Quotient Rule: $\left(\dfrac{f(x)}{g(x)}\right)'=\dfrac{f'(x)\cdot g(x)-g'(x)\cdot f(x)}{g^{2}(x)}$
$\left(\sin x\right)'=\cos x$	Chain Rule: $\left(f\left(g(x)\right)\right)'=f'\left(g(x)\right)\cdot g'(x)$
$\left(\cos x\right)'=-\sin x$	$\left(a\right)'=0$
$\left(\tan x\right)'=\sec^{2} x$	$\left(x\right)'=1$
$\left(\cot x\right)'=-\csc^{2} x$	$\left(e^{x}\right)'=e^{x}$
$\left(\sec x\right)'=\sec x\tan x$	$\left(\ln x\right)'=\dfrac{1}{x}$
$\left(\csc x\right)'=-\csc x\cot x$	$\left(a^{x}\right)'=a^{x}\ln a,\ a>0,\ a\neq 1$
$\left(\sin^{-1} x\right)'=\dfrac{1}{\sqrt{1-x^{2}}}$	$\left(\log_{a} x\right)'=\dfrac{1}{x\ln a}$
$\left(\tan^{-1} x\right)'=\dfrac{1}{1+x^{2}}$	$\left(\sqrt{x}\right)'=\dfrac{1}{2\sqrt{x}}$
$\left(\sec^{-1} x\right)'=\dfrac{1}{x\sqrt{x^{2}-1}}$	$\left(\dfrac{1}{x}\right)'=-\dfrac{1}{x^{2}}$

Formulas and Theorems

Integration Formulas

$\int \sin x \, dx = -\cos x + C$	$\int x^n dx = \dfrac{x^{n+1}}{n+1} + C, \; n \neq -1$
$\int \cos x \, dx = \sin x + C$	$\int a \, dx = ax + C$
$\int \tan x \, dx = -\ln|\cos x| + C \text{ or } \ln|\sec x| + C$	$\int e^x \, dx = e^x + C$
$\int \cot x \, dx = \ln|\sin x| + C \text{ or } -\ln|\csc x| + C$	$\int a^x dx = \dfrac{a^x}{\ln a} + C$
$\int \sec x \, dx = \ln|\sec x + \tan x| + C$	$\int \dfrac{1}{x} dx = \ln|x| + C$
$\int \csc x \, dx = \ln|\csc x - \cot x| + C$	$\int \dfrac{1}{\sqrt{a^2 - x^2}} dx = \sin^{-1}\dfrac{x}{a} + C$
$\int \sec x \tan x \, dx = \sec x + C$	$\int \dfrac{1}{a^2 + x^2} dx = \dfrac{1}{a}\tan^{-1}\dfrac{x}{a} + C$
$\int \csc x \cot x \, dx = -\csc x + C$	$\int \dfrac{1}{x\sqrt{x^2 - a^2}} dx = \dfrac{1}{a}\sec^{-1}\dfrac{x}{a} + C$
$\int \sec^2 x \, dx = \tan x + C$	$\int \csc^2 x \, dx = -\cot x + C$

Continuity	A function $f(x)$ is continuous at $x = a$ if all of the following are true: I. $f(a)$ exists II. $\lim\limits_{x \to a} f(x)$ exists III. $\lim\limits_{x \to a} f(x) = f(a)$
Intermediate Value Theorem	If function $f(x)$ is continuous on a closed interval $[a,b]$ and if w is any number between $f(a)$ and $f(b)$, then there is at least one number c in $[a,b]$ such that $f(c) = w$
Limit Theorem	$\lim\limits_{x \to a} f(x) = L$ if and only if $\lim\limits_{x \to a^+} f(x) = L = \lim\limits_{x \to a^-} f(x)$

Formulas and Theorems

Vertical Asymptote	A line $x = a$ is a vertical asymptote of the graph of a function $y = f(x)$ if $\lim\limits_{x \to a^+} f(x) = \pm\infty$ or $\lim\limits_{x \to a^-} f(x) = \pm\infty$
Horizontal Asymptote	A line $y = L$ is a horizontal asymptote of the graph of a function $f(x)$ if $\lim\limits_{x \to \infty} f(x) = L$ or $\lim\limits_{x \to -\infty} f(x) = L$
Average Rate of Change	Average rate of change of $y = f(x)$ on $[a, a+h]$ is $\dfrac{f(a+h) - f(a)}{h}$
Instantaneous Rate of Change	Instantaneous rate of change of $y = f(x)$ on $[a, a+h]$ is: $\lim\limits_{h \to 0}\left(\text{Average rate of change}\right) = \lim\limits_{h \to 0} \dfrac{f(a+h) - f(a)}{h}$
Sandwich Theorem	If $f(x) \le g(x) \le h(x)$ for all $x \ne c$ in some interval about c, and $\lim\limits_{x \to c} f(x) = \lim\limits_{x \to c} h(x) = L$, then $\lim\limits_{x \to c} g(x) = L$
Definition of Derivative	$f'(x) = \lim\limits_{h \to 0} \dfrac{f(x+h) - f(x)}{h}$ or $f'(x) = \lim\limits_{x \to c} \dfrac{f(x) - f(c)}{x - c}$
Theorem	If a function $f(x)$ is differentiable at $x = a$, then it is continuous at $x = a$
Differentiability on a closed interval	A function f is differentiable on a closed interval $[a, b]$ if f is differentiable on the open interval (a, b) and if both Right-Hand Derivative at a and Left-Hand Derivative at b exist
Rolle's Theorem	Suppose that $f(x)$ is continuous on the closed interval $[a, b]$ and differentiable on the open interval (a, b). If $f(a) = f(b)$, then there is at least one number c between a and b such that $f'(c) = 0$
Mean Value Theorem	If $f(x)$ is continuous on the closed interval $[a, b]$ and differentiable on the open interval (a, b), then there is at least one number c between a and b such that $f'(c) = \dfrac{f(b) - f(a)}{b - a}$
Derivative of the Inverse function	If g is the inverse function of a differentiable function f and if $f'(g(x)) \ne 0$, then $g'(x) = \dfrac{1}{f'(g(x))}$
Linear approximation of f(x) near x = x₀	$y = f(x_0) + f'(x_0)(x - x_0)$

Formulas and Theorems

Extrema and Concavity

Critical Numbers (Candidates for Extrema)	A number c in the domain of a function f is a critical number of f if either $f'(c)=0$ or $f'(c)$ does not exist
Increasing/Decreasing Functions	If $f(x)$ is differentiable on (a,b) and continuous on $[a,b]$: $f'(x)>0$ on $(a,b) \Rightarrow f(x)$ is increasing on $[a,b]$ $f'(x)<0$ on $(a,b) \Rightarrow f(x)$ is deccreasing on $[a,b]$
Local Minimum	$f(c)$ is the local minimum value of f if $f(c) \leq f(x)$ for every x in an interval I around c
Local Maximum	$f(c)$ is the local maximum value of f if $f(c) \geq f(x)$ for every x in an interval I around c
Absolute Minimum	$f(c)$ is the absolute minimum value of f if $f(c) \leq f(x)$ for every x in the domain of f
Absolute Maximum	$f(c)$ is the absolute maximum value of f if $f(c) \geq f(x)$ for every x in the domain of f
Finding the Absolute Extrema on [a,b]	1. Find Critical numbers. 2. Calculate the function values at the endpoints of $[a,b]$ and at the critical numbers. 3. The largest of these function values is the absolute maximum The smallest function value is the absolute minimum.
Finding the Local Extrema (First Derivative Test)	Find critical numbers $x=c$ $\left(\text{where } f'(c)=0 \text{ or DNE}\right)$ Local minimum occurs at $x=c$, where $f'(x)$ changes from negative to positive. Local maximum occurs at $x=c$, where $f'(x)$ changes from positive to negative.
Concavity	If $f''(x)$ exists on (a,b), then: $f''(x)>0 \Rightarrow f(x)$ concave upward in (a,b) $f''(x)<0 \Rightarrow f(x)$ concave downward in (a,b)
Points of Inflection	Points of Inflection of $f(x)$ are the points on the Domain of $f(x)$ where $f''(x)=0$ or DNE and $f''(x)$ changes its sign passing through them.
Extreme Value Theorem	If f is continuous on a closed interval $[a,b]$, then f has both an absolute minimum and an absolute maximum value on $[a,b]$

Formulas and Theorems

Integrals

Definite Integral. Property 1	$\int_a^b c \cdot f(x)dx = c\int_a^b f(x)dx$
Definite Integral. Property 2	$\int_a^b f(x)dx = -\int_b^a f(x)dx$
Definite Integral. Property 3	$\int_a^a f(x)dx = 0$
Definite Integral. Property 4	If f is integrable on a closed interval and if a, b and c are any three numbers in the interval, then $\int_a^b f(x)dx = \int_a^c f(x)dx + \int_c^b f(x)dx$
If $f(x) \geq 0$ on $[a,b]$:	If $f(x) \geq 0$ on $[a,b]$ then $\int_a^b f(x)dx \geq 0$
If $g(x) \geq f(x)$ on $[a, b]$:	If $g(x) \geq f(x)$ on $[a, b]$ then $\int_a^b f(x)dx \geq 0$
If f(x) is an even function:	If f is an Even Function, then $\int_{-a}^a f(x)dx = 2\int_0^a f(x)dx$
If f(x) is an odd function:	If f is an Odd Function, then $\int_{-a}^a f(x)dx = 0$
Riemann sum	Let $f(x)$ be defined on a closed interval $[a,b]$ and P is any decomposition of $[a,b]$ into subintervals of the form $[x_{k-1}, x_k]$. Riemann sum of $f(x)$ for P is $R_P = \sum_{k=1}^n f(w_k)\Delta x_k$ where $w_k \in [x_{k-1}, x_k]$.
Integral as limit of Riemann sums	The definite integral of f from a to b, $\int_a^b f(x)dx = \lim_{\|p\|\to 0}\sum_k f(w_k)\Delta x_k$ provided the limit exists where $\|p\|$ is the norm of the partition (largest Δx_k)
Integral as area under the curve	If f is integrable and $f(x) \geq 0$ for every x in $[a,b]$ (where $a < b$), then the area A of the region under the graph of f from a to b is $A = \int_a^b f(x)dx$
Fundamental Theorem of Calculus	$\dfrac{d}{dx}\int_a^x f(t)dt = f(x)$ and $\int_a^b f'(x)dx = f(b) - f(a)$
Velocity	$v(t) = x'(t)$ $v(t) = \int a(t)dt$

Formulas and Theorems

Acceleration	$a(t) = v'(t) = x''(t)$
Speed. Increasing and Decreasing Speed	Speed $= |v(t)|$ Velocity and acceleration have the same signs $\Rightarrow$ speed increases Velocity and acceleration have the opposite signs $\Rightarrow$ speed decreases
Position	$x(t) = \int v(t)\,dt$
Average Velocity	$v_{av} = \dfrac{s(t_2) - s(t_1)}{t_2 - t_1}$
Instantaneous velocity	$v_{inst} = \lim\limits_{t_2 \to t_1} \dfrac{s(t_2) - s(t_1)}{t_2 - t_1}$
Total Distance	Total Distance $= \int_a^b |v(t)|\,dt$
Net Change or Displacement	Net Change (or Displacement) $= \int_a^b v(t)\,dt$
Area between the curves	$A = \int_a^b \big(f(x) - g(x)\big)\,dx$, where $f(x) > g(x)$ on $[a,b]$
Volume by Disks	$V = \pi \int_a^b R^2\,dx$ (if region is rotating around horizontal line) or: $V = \pi \int_c^d R^2\,dy$ (if region is rotating around vertical line)
Volume by Washers	$V = \pi \int_a^b \big(R^2 - r^2\big)\,dx$ (if region is rotating around horizontal line) or: $V = \pi \int_c^d \big(R^2 - r^2\big)\,dy$ (if region is rotating around vertical line)
Volume by Cross Sections	$V = \int_a^b A(x)\,dx$ (if the cross sections are $\perp$ to x-axis) or: $V = \int_c^d A(y)\,dy$ (if the cross sections are $\perp$ to y-axis)
Average value of f	Average Value of $f(x)$ on $[a,b]$ is: $f_{av} = \dfrac{1}{b-a} \int_a^b f(x)\,dx$
Arc Length	Arc Length: $L = \int_a^b \sqrt{1 + \big[f'(x)\big]^2}\,dx$ or: $L = \int_c^d \sqrt{1 + \big[g'(y)\big]^2}\,dy$

Formulas and Theorems

Integration by parts	If $u = f(x)$ and $v = g(x)$ and if f' and g' are continuous, then $\int u\,dv = uv - \int v\,du$
L'Hospital's Rule	If $\lim\limits_{x \to c} \dfrac{f(x)}{g(x)}$ is of the form $\dfrac{0}{0}$ or $\dfrac{\infty}{\infty}$, then $\lim\limits_{x \to c} \dfrac{f(x)}{g(x)} = \lim\limits_{x \to c} \dfrac{f'(x)}{g'(x)}$, provided either $\lim\limits_{x \to c} \dfrac{f'(x)}{g'(x)}$ exists or $\lim\limits_{x \to c} \dfrac{f'(x)}{g'(x)} = \infty$
Improper Integrals	If $f(x)$ is continuous on $[a, \infty)$, then $\int_a^\infty f(x)\,dx = \lim\limits_{t \to \infty} \int_a^t f(x)\,dx$ If $f(x)$ is continuous on $[-\infty, a)$, then $\int_{-\infty}^a f(x)\,dx = \lim\limits_{t \to -\infty} \int_t^a f(x)\,dx$
Improper Integrals	If $f(x)$ is continuous on $(a, b]$ and discontinuous at a, then $\int_a^b f(x)\,dx = \lim\limits_{t \to a^+} \int_t^b f(x)\,dx$ If $f(x)$ is continuous on $[a, b)$ and discontinuous at b, then $\int_a^b f(x)\,dx = \lim\limits_{t \to b^-} \int_a^t f(x)\,dx$ If $f(x)$ has discontinuity at a number c in the interval (a, b), but continuous elsewhere on $[a, b]$, then $\int_a^b f(x)\,dx = \int_a^c f(x)\,dx + \int_c^b f(x)\,dx$

Parametric Equations and Polar coordinates

Derivative of a function given parametrically	$\dfrac{dy}{dx} = \dfrac{\frac{dy}{dt}}{\frac{dx}{dt}}$
Second derivative of a function given parametrically	$\dfrac{d^2 y}{dx^2} = \dfrac{\frac{dy'}{dt}}{\frac{dx}{dt}}$
Arc Length of a curve given parametrically	$L = \int_a^b \sqrt{\left[f'(t)\right]^2 + \left[g'(t)\right]^2}\,dt = \int_a^b \sqrt{\left(\dfrac{dx}{dt}\right)^2 + \left(\dfrac{dy}{dt}\right)^2}\,dt$
Polar to Cartesian	$x = r\cos\theta \quad y = r\sin\theta$
Cartesian to Polar	$x^2 + y^2 = r^2 \qquad \tan\theta = \dfrac{y}{x}$
Area in polar coordinates	If f is continuous and $f(\theta) \geq 0$ on $[\alpha, \beta]$, where $0 \leq \alpha < \beta \leq 2\pi$, then the area A of the region bounded by the graphs of $r = f(\theta)$, $\theta = \alpha$, and $\theta = \beta$ is $A = \dfrac{1}{2}\int_\alpha^\beta r^2\,d\theta = \dfrac{1}{2}\int_\alpha^\beta (f(\theta))^2\,d\theta$
Area between the curves	$A = \dfrac{1}{2}\int_\alpha^\beta \left(r_2^2 - r_1^2\right)d\theta$

Formulas and Theorems

Vectors

Position: $s(t) = \langle x(t), y(t) \rangle$
Velocity: $v(t) = s'(t) = \left\langle \dfrac{dx}{dt}, \dfrac{dy}{dt} \right\rangle$
Speed: $\|v(t)\| = \sqrt{\left(\dfrac{dx}{dt}\right)^2 + \left(\dfrac{dy}{dt}\right)^2}$
Acceleration: $a(t) = v'(t) = s''(t) = \left\langle \dfrac{d^2x}{dt^2}, \dfrac{d^2y}{dt^2} \right\rangle$

Sequences and Series

Sequence	If a sequence $\{a_n\}$ has a limit L $\left(\lim\limits_{n\to\infty} a_n = L\right)$, then a sequence is said to converge to L. If there is no limit, the sequence diverges.
Sandwich Theorem	If $\{a_n\}, \{b_n\}$ and $\{c_n\}$ are sequences and $a_n \le b_n \le c_n$ for every n and if $\lim\limits_{n\to\infty} a_n = L = \lim\limits_{n\to\infty} c_n$, then $\lim\limits_{n\to\infty} b_n = L$
Theorem	Series $\sum a_n$ converges if sequence of partial sums $\{S_n\}$ converges
Harmonic Series	The Harmonic Series $\sum\limits_{n=1}^{\infty} \dfrac{1}{n} = 1 + \dfrac{1}{2} + \dfrac{1}{3} + \ldots + \dfrac{1}{n} + \ldots$ diverges

Geometric Series	Geometric Series : $a + ar + ar^2 + \ldots + ar^n + \ldots \quad (a \ne 0)$
	
	     I. Converges and has the sum $S = \dfrac{a}{1-r}$ if $\|r\| < 1$
	
	     II. Diverges if $\|r\| \ge 1$

Nth Term Test for divergence	(I) If $\lim\limits_{n\to\infty} a_n \ne 0$, the series $\sum a_n$ is divergent. (II) If $\lim\limits_{n\to\infty} a_n = 0$, investigate further
Theorem	For any positive integer k, the series $\sum\limits_{n=1}^{\infty} a_n = a_1 + a_2 + \ldots$ and $\sum\limits_{n=k+1}^{\infty} a_n = a_{k+1} + a_{k+2} + \ldots$ either both converge or both diverge

Formulas and Theorems

Theorem	If $\sum a_n$ and $\sum b_n$ are convergent series with sums A and B, respectively, then I. $\sum (a_n + b_n)$ converges and has a sum $A + B$ II. $\sum c a_n$ converges and has a sum cA for every real number c III. $\sum (a_n - b_n)$ converges and has a sum $A - B$
Theorem	If $\sum a_n$ is a convergent series and $\sum b_n$ is divergent, then $\sum (a_n + b_n)$ is divergent
Integral Test	Suppose $f(x)$ is a continuous, positive, decreasing function on $[1, \infty)$ and let $a_n = f(n)$. Then the series $\sum_{n=1}^{\infty} a_n$ and the improper integral $\int_1^{\infty} f(x)\, dx$ both converge or both diverge.
P-Series	The p-series $\sum_{n=1}^{\infty} \dfrac{1}{n^p} = 1 + \dfrac{1}{2^p} + \dfrac{1}{3^p} + \ldots + \dfrac{1}{n^p} + \ldots$ converges if $p > 1$ and diverges if $p \le 1$
Basic Comparison Test	Let $\sum a_n$ and $\sum b_n$ be positive-term series. If $\sum b_n$ converges and $a_n \le b_n$ then $\sum a_n$ also converges. If $\sum b_n$ diverges and $a_n \ge b_n$ then $\sum a_n$ also diverges.
Limit Comparison Test	Let $\sum a_n$ and $\sum b_n$ be positive-term series. If $\lim\limits_{n \to \infty} \dfrac{a_n}{b_n} = c > 0$ then either both series converge or both diverge.
Alternating Series Test	The alternating series $\sum_{n=1}^{\infty} (-1)^{n-1} a_n = a_1 - a_2 + a_3 - \ldots + (-1)^{n-1} a_n + \ldots$ is convergent if I. $a_k \ge a_{k+1} > 0$ for every k II. $\lim\limits_{n \to \infty} a_n = 0$
Error Theorem for Alternating series	Let $\sum_{n=1}^{\infty} (-1)^{n-1} a_n$ be Convergent Alternating Series. If S is the sum of the series and S_n is a partial sum, then $$|S - S_n| \le a_{n+1}$$ that is, the error involved in approximating S by S_n, $|E| \le a_{n+1}$
Absolutely Convergent Series	$\sum a_n$ is absolutely convergent if the series $\sum |a_n| = |a_1| + |a_2| + \ldots + |a_n| + \ldots$ is convergent
Conditionally Convergent Series	$\sum a_n$ is conditionally convergent if $\sum a_n$ is convergent and $\sum |a_n|$ is divergent.
Theorem	If a series $\sum a_n$ is absolutely convergent, then $\sum a_n$ is convergent.

Formulas and Theorems

Ratio Test	Let $\sum a_n$ be a series with non-zero terms and suppose $\lim\limits_{n\to\infty}\left\|\dfrac{a_{n+1}}{a_n}\right\| = L$ I. If $L < 1$, series converges absolutely II. If $L > 1$ or $\lim\limits_{n\to\infty}\left\|\dfrac{a_{n+1}}{a_n}\right\| = \infty$, series diverges III. If $L = 1$, then the test is inconclusive and different test must be used.
Power Series in x	A power series in x is a series of the form $\sum\limits_{n=0}^{\infty} a_n x^n = a_0 + a_1 x + a_2 x^2 + \ldots + a_n x^n + \ldots$, where each a_k is a real number.
Power Series in x-c	A power series in $x - c$ is a series of the form $\sum\limits_{n=0}^{\infty} a_n (x-c)^n = a_0 + a_1(x-c) + a_2(x-c)^2 + \ldots + a_n(x-c)^n + \ldots$, where each a_k and c are real numbers.
Interval of convergence	The set of all numbers x for which the power series converges is called the Interval of Convergence
Radius of convergence	If a power series centered at $x = c$ converges when $\|x - c\| < R$ and diverges when $\|x - c\| > R$, then the value of R is called the Radius of Convergence
Frequently Used Series	$\dfrac{1}{1-x} = 1 + x + x^2 + x^3 + \ldots + x^n + \ldots = \sum\limits_{n=0}^{\infty} x^n, \; \|x\| < 1$ $e^x = 1 + x + \dfrac{x^2}{2!} + \dfrac{x^3}{3!} + \ldots + \dfrac{x^n}{n!} + \ldots = \sum\limits_{n=0}^{\infty} \dfrac{x^n}{n!}, \; \|x\| < \infty$ $\sin x = x - \dfrac{x^3}{3!} + \dfrac{x^5}{5!} - \dfrac{x^7}{7!} + \ldots + (-1)^n \dfrac{x^{2n+1}}{(2n+1)!} + \ldots = \sum\limits_{n=0}^{\infty} \dfrac{(-1)^n x^{2n+1}}{(2n+1)!}, \; \|x\| < \infty$ $\cos x = 1 - \dfrac{x^2}{2!} + \dfrac{x^4}{4!} - \ldots + \dfrac{(-1)^n x^{2n}}{(2n)!} + \ldots = \sum\limits_{n=0}^{\infty} \dfrac{(-1)^n x^{2n}}{(2n)!}, \; \|x\| < \infty$
Maclaurin Series or Taylor Series at x=0	$f(x) = \sum\limits_{n=0}^{\infty} \dfrac{f^{(n)}(0)}{n!} x^n = f(0) + f'(0)x + \dfrac{f''(0)}{2!}x^2 + \dfrac{f'''(0)}{3!}x^3 + \ldots + \dfrac{f^{(n)}(0)}{n!}x^n + \ldots$ where f is the function which has derivatives of all orders throughout some interval containing $x = 0$.
Taylor Series at x=a	$f(x) = \sum\limits_{n=0}^{\infty} \dfrac{f^{(n)}(a)}{n!} (x-a)^n = f(a) + f'(a)(x-a) + \dfrac{f''(a)}{2!}(x-a)^2 + \ldots + \dfrac{f^{(n)}(a)}{n!}(x-a)^n + \ldots$ where f is the function which has derivatives of all orders throughout some interval containing $x = a$.
Lagrange Error Bound	$\text{Error} \leq \|R_n(x)\| = \left\|\dfrac{f^{(n+1)}(c)}{(n+1)!}(x-a)^{n+1}\right\|$ where c is between x and a.

Tips for the AP Test

- Functions could have various notations such as: $Si(x), erf(x)$

- Don't cross out your work unless you know you can do better. But if you make a mistake, cross it out. A crossed out solution is not graded.

- If you are afraid your result is wrong in Part A, use it anyway to finish the problem.

- Don't write $f(x) = 2(1.5) + 3$ when you mean $f(1.5) = 2(1.5) + 3$.

- Name the function you are referring to. Not "its slope is…" but "the slope of g is…" when more than one function is being used.

- If you are being asked to set up an integral and you are not sure about integrand, start with at least the limits of integration and constant in front of it and make a guess at the integrand.

- Know the difference between local (relative) and global (absolute) extrema.

- Know the difference between the **extreme value** and the **location** of the extreme value. If they ask you to "find the *minimum*", they want the *y-value*. If they ask, "At which *x* does this function have a minimum?" they want the *x-value*. If they ask, "At which *point* does this function have a minimum?" they want *both coordinates (x,y)*.

- Know the difference between a **point in time** and an **interval of time**. "During, before", "within", "after", and "until" are intervals. "At" or "when" indicate a point in time!

- If you use a rule, show how it applies to the given problem. Generic theorems or procedures get no credit. Don't write "By Mean Value Theorem" etc.; instead explain how the conditions and rules apply to your problem.

- Volume problems that are given **will not** require use of the **Shell method**. Shell method can be used, but problem could also be solved using Disc, Washers, or Cross Section method.

- If in Washer method you write $(f(x) - g(x))^2$ vs. $(f(x))^2 - (g(x))^2$ you might **LOSE ALL POINTS & NOT BE GIVEN ANY PARTIAL CREDIT.**

- In rotation problems, when the solid is rotating around a Horizontal line *y* = 2, or Vertical line *x* = 1, be careful about rotating the figure around the **correct** line.

- Answers have to be reasonable. If you make a mistake in finding the area under the curve, and the answer is negative, it is UNREASONABLE. You can lose points for such errors and NOT BE GIVEN PARTIAL CREDIT.

- If you have "=" sign make sure that left is equal to the right. Don't put something like $2 + 5 = 7 + 1 = 8$. Instead put $2 + 5 = 7$; $7 + 1 = 8$.

- Point-slope form of an equation, $y - y_0 = m(x - x_0)$, is perfectly acceptable. There is no need to simplify it into $y = mx + b$ form. The form $\dfrac{y - y_0}{x - x_0} = m$ is not acceptable because of the restrictions for the denominator.

- Answers like $2 + \sin\dfrac{\pi}{3}$, $2 + \tan^{-1} 1$, $\dfrac{(.1)^2 x^2}{2!} + \dfrac{(.1)^3 x^3}{3!}$ are acceptable. You don't have to simplify it anymore.

- When use trapezoidal approximation, your answer is a complicated sum. Leave it as a sum, like 2.71 + 3.06 + 5.06. You don't have to do the arithmetic and add the terms up

- THEY DON'T ACCEPT diagrams for justification of local maximum, local minimum, and concavity. Instead you need to write the explanation similar to: **Local minimum occurs at x = 3, because that's where derivative of *f*** (or *g* or *h* etc.) **changes from negative to positive.**

- For every part of the free response, give all the answers with at least 3 digits after the decimal point, rounded or truncated. More is okay. Make sure the numbers you are using for earlier steps of the solution contain MORE THAN 3 digits after the decimal point. Don't round too soon, or else your answer may be off.

- When graphing the slope field (direction fields), extend it all the way through the given window.

- When using L'Hospital's Rule, consider limits of denominator and numerator separately and DO NOT write "$= \dfrac{0}{0}$" or "$= \dfrac{\infty}{\infty}$"

- When use a table for the Euler's method, make sure to write all names of each field on your header row completely: x; old y; $\Delta y = \dfrac{dy}{dx} \cdot \Delta x$; new $y = $ old $y + \Delta y$. Otherwise your work will not be accepted.

- When finding Error for alternating series, first prove that the series is convergent by alternating series test, and then find the Error.

Answer Key

Exam 1	Exam 2	Exam 3	Exam 4	Exam 5	Exam 6
1) C	1) C	1) C	1) B	1) D	1) B
2) A	2) A	2) B	2) D	2) D	2) B
3) B	3) C	3) B	3) D	3) D	3) B
4) C	4) B	4) A	4) A	4) C	4) D
5) A	5) D	5) A	5) C	5) D	5) C
6) C	6) D	6) A	6) A	6) B	6) A
7) A	7) C	7) A	7) B	7) C	7) B
8) C	8) D	8) B	8) C	8) A	8) A
9) A	9) C	9) A	9) A	9) D	9) D
10) B	10) B	10) B	10) B	10) C	10) A
11) A	11) C	11) C	11) A	11) A	11) D
12) B	12) D	12) B	12) A	12) C	12) A
13) D	13) C	13) D	13) B	13) C	13) C
14) C	14) A	14) B	14) A	14) A	14) B
15) D	15) D	15) C	15) A	15) D	15) A
16) A	16) C	16) D	16) A	16) D	16) C
17) C	17) C	17) A	17) A	17) A	17) B
18) A	18) C	18) C	18) D	18) A	18) C
19) C	19) C	19) A	19) C	19) D	19) C
20) D	20) D	20) A	20) C	20) D	20) C
21) D	21) A	21) C	21) B	21) B	21) C
22) B	22) C	22) A	22) C	22) B	22) A
23) B	23) B	23) A	23) C	23) D	23) A
24) B	24) B	24) D	24) A	24) A	24) D
25) B	25) D	25) A	25) B	25) B	25) C
26) D	26) D	26) B	26) A	26) C	26) A
27) A	27) C	27) D	27) B	27) C	27) D
28) B	28) A	28) A	28) C	28) C	28) C
29) B	29) C	29) A	29) D	29) C	29) A
30) B	30) D	30) B	30) D	30) B	30) C
31) C	31) C	31) D	31) A	31) B	31) C
32) A	32) D	32) C	32) C	32) B	32) A
33) B	33) D	33) A	33) C	33) B	33) A
34) B	34) B	34) A	34) D	34) B	34) A
35) D	35) B	35) B	35) A	35) C	35) A
36) C	36) B	36) B	36) C	36) C	36) A
37) B	37) B	37) A	37) D	37) B	37) B
38) A	38) C	38) A	38) B	38) D	38) B
39) C	39) C	39) B	39) B	39) C	39) A
40) D	40) B	40) A	40) C	40) D	40) A
41) C	41) D	41) C	41) D	41) A	41) B
42) B	42) B	42) A	42) C	42) B	42) C
43) C	43) C	43) D	43) B	43) B	43) C
44) C	44) A	44) A	44) C	44) D	44) A
45) B	45) C	45) B	45) C	45) A	45) D

Made in the USA
Monee, IL
07 April 2021

64980901R10090